LAND OF NINE DRAGONS

PHOTOGRAPHS BY

NEVADA WIER

TEXT BY

JOSEPH R. YOGERST

LAND OF
NINE DRAGONS:
VIETNAM TODAY

ABBEVILLE PRESS PUBLISHERS

NEW YORK-LONDON-PARIS

Editor: Walton Rawls
Designer: Nai Chang
Copy chief: Robin James
Production supervisor: Hope Koturo

FRONT COVER:
Fishermen on Xuan Huong Lake, early morning, Dalat, Lam Dong province. See page 144.

BACK COVER:
Entrance to an old shrine in Hoan Kiem district, Hanoi. See page 18.

FRONTISPIECE:
Black Thai girl poses with lau flower bundles, Son La province.

PAGE 6; CLOCKWISE FROM TOP LEFT:
Young Black Thai girl on the road to Son La province from Dien Bien Phu.

Black Thai women returning home from work, Dien Bien Phu, Lai Chau province.

White Thai villager, Lat village, Lai Chau province. See page 72.

Young Black Thai boy, Dien Bien Phu, Lai Chau province.

Black Thai headman of Tong Nho village, Son La province, with his wife and fortune book.

White Thai woman crossing bamboo bridge, Son La province.

Library of Congress Cataloging-in-Publication Data

Yogerst, Joseph R.
    Land of nine dragons : Vietnam today / photographs by Nevada Wier; text by Joseph R. Yogerst.
        p.   cm.
    Includes index.
    ISBN 1-55859-221-0
    1. Vietnam—Description and travel—1975– 2. Vietnam—Pictorial works.   I. Wier, Nevada.
    DS556.39.Y64   1992   92-22992
    915.9704'44'0222—dc20   CIP

Abbeville Publishing Group,
488 Madison Avenue,
New York, NY 10022

Printed and bound in Japan
First edition

Photographer's Foreword

"Vietnam." The very name conjures a myriad of feelings. Twenty-five years ago I was too young to fully comprehend the traumas and passions evoked by the Vietnam War, yet there is no escaping the impact Vietnam has had on America's cultural psyche.

I remember my first day in Hanoi. I was alone in a new country; I knew no one and had the tremendous responsibility of a book project and no idea how to begin it. I was wandering through the warren of streets in Hoan Kiem district when an old woman stopped me and asked in a questioning voice, "Lienxo?" (Russian). I hesitated, shook my head and replied with one of the few Vietnamese words I had learned, "My" (American). She threw back her head, laughed, and gave me a big thumbs-up sign. I was stunned—and relieved. I realized how anxious I was and afraid of the reception I, an American, might be given. From that moment I relaxed and approached Vietnam as I would any foreign country—with curiosity, respect, openness, and a fresh mind.

Although I traveled extensively in Vietnam, visiting the country five times during a period of one year, there are still many places I would have liked to visit, people I wish I had met. My photography propelled me closer to its heart, but it is a journey still unfinished.

The Vietnamese are trying desperately to bridge their differences with the United States. My hope is that soon America will mend its wounds and come to see Vietnam not as a war, but a country.

I am indebted to numerous people for their help and support. I particularly want to thank everyone at the Foreign Press Center in Hanoi for their patience and effort, including Nguyen Cong Quang and Nguyen Van Thuan. Tran Van Khoa deserves a special mention as my friend, translator, and companion on the majority of my travels in Vietnam. I also want to thank Nguyen Quang Dy at the Vietnam Embassy in Bangkok.

I was warmly welcomed in all the provinces and cities of Vietnam and wish to extend my gratitude to everyone who graciously invited me, and my camera, into their lives. Nguyen Tran Bat, Dam Bich Thuy, and all the staff of InvestConsult merit a warm thanks for their sympathetic assistance and friendship from the very beginning of my endeavors.

Most importantly, I thank my friends, Sally Butler, Shelly O'Connell, Jean Farhood, Heather Massey, Robert Horgan, Orawan, Wippan Herman, Tom Seale, Mike and Caddy Chaddick, Landt and Lisl Dennis, Zenia Victor, Galen Duke, Steve Van Beek, Joe Yogerst, John Dillon, Richard Hughes, and, most of all, Charles Granatir. Without their compassion and support, I never would have finished this project.

—Nevada Wier

Author's Foreword

Most accounts of contemporary Vietnam take the retrospective approach: veterans or correspondents returning for the first time since the war, comparing what they see today with their memories of combat. They dwell on the past, on the historical perspective, but they tell us little of the place and people as they exist in the 1990s.

My objective with *Land of Nine Dragons* was to take a much different look at Vietnam, to examine the nation as a modern entity rather than as a segment of American military history or a personal memoir.

Of course, there's no way that I could entirely divorce myself from the war experience. I wasn't old enough to have been a reporter or a soldier. But I grew up with Vietnam—as surely as I was raised with baseball or the Beatles or Disneyland. You couldn't avoid it as a kid in America. It was there in the living room each night, Walter Cronkite relating the latest gruesome details on the *CBS Evening News*. It was in the papers too, and in the popular music of the time. Much later, as a young adult, I could experience the war at the detached level of a film or book.

But no matter how much I tried, I could never relate to Vietnam in the same way as someone who had been there during the war. Instead, I set out to clear away the clouds of war and discover the essence of modern Vietnam.

What is Vietnam today? A nation of roughly seventy million people, most of them ethnic Viets, but with a significant number of hilltribe minorities. An S-shaped country that snakes its way down the Indochina coast, anchored by Hanoi in the north and Ho Chi Minh City (Saigon) in the south. An incredibly diverse landscape that ranges from tropical beaches and mangrove swamp to picture postcard rice paddies and impenetrable rainforest. One of Asia's least developed economies, but a place at which American, Japanese, and European investors are casting a sharp eye. A Communist state, but with a government that is under rising pressure to reform in terms of both economic policy and basic human rights.

While the book is not in itself a political statement, I hope it provides a vehicle for mutual understanding. Showing Vietnam in a 1990s context—the culture, the geography, the resources, the landscapes, and the people—is especially important given the recent thaw in United States–Vietnamese relations. Washington's volte-face on the Cambodia issue and Hanoi's more constructive attitude on MIAs have opened the door for the first direct talks between the respective governments since 1975, paving the way for the end of the American-sponsored trade embargo and the resumption of normal diplomatic ties.

Many international and domestic obstacles must still be overcome before Vietnam can take its place as a full partner in Southeast Asia's politics and economy. But it's important for all concerned parties to start thinking of Vietnam as a nation rather than a hideous war.

—Joseph Yogerst

CONTENTS

People said it wasn't the best time to be going to Vietnam. Indeed, from the perspective of the outside world—even from the close proximity of Bangkok—it seemed that Vietnam in the summer of 1990 was on the verge of upheaval. The months leading up to my visit were charged with internal strife, and stress was also being applied from several foreign quarters.

Mikhail Gorbachev's *perestroika* in the Soviet Union and the rapid disintegration of Communism in Eastern Europe were having unexpected ramifications in Vietnam. Moscow and the other Iron Curtain regimes were severing their military ties and ending their once-plentiful handouts to Hanoi. Thousands of Vietnamese workers had returned from factories in Germany, Hungary, and Czechoslovakia, made redundant by new democratic governments that would not tolerate the near slave-labor conditions under which the Vietnamese had worked. Relations remained chilly with China, too. It seemed that the whole of Communism had turned its back on Vietnam, left it to fend for itself in a region where the domino theory had been immovably reversed in favor of free enterprise. The irony was not lost on the Vietnamese, who were now scrambling for new friends.

Yet events were not auspicious on the capitalist front either. Despite the well-publicized withdrawal from Cambodia and other atonements to meet American demands, Hanoi had seen no discernible change in its relationship with Washington. The American economic and diplomatic embargo—imposed in 1975 after the North had breached the Paris Peace Accord with its invasion of the South—was still rock solid. Policy in Washington was showing no signs of fracture, and as a result other potential "friends" were staying at arm's

The banner of the Socialist Republic of Vietnam flies high over Ba Dinh Square and the Mausoleum of Ho Chi Minh. Inside the stark cement tomb is Ho's body, encased in a glass coffin. Each day thousands of Vietnamese make the pilgrimage to the tomb.

In what could easily be a scene from old Paris, the pervasive influence of French Belle Epoque design on public architecture in Hanoi can be seen in this ornate wrought-iron gate at the entrance to the former University of Indochina in Hai Ba Trung district. The structure now houses the Hanoi Polytechnic University.

length, particularly Japan. The conventional wisdom among Vietnamese was that their economy would shift into overdrive as soon as the American embargo lapsed. They waited expectantly, gazing with increasing envy at the booming economies of Southeast Asia—Thailand, Malaysia, Singapore, and Hong Kong—and eventually they became angry. So angry, they began to lash out at anything that smacked of dissent or treason.

Just prior to my arrival, an American businessman had been arrested and detained in Da Nang under what appeared to be flimsy charges. After being held for three weeks, the businessman and his French partner were deported. An American teacher—a young Mennonite woman—was expelled for using "seditious" learning materials. The offensive documents turned out to be clippings from American newspapers used in instructing high-school English students. It wasn't just foreigners. Five Vietnamese writers and half a dozen people who helped smuggle their works abroad had been arrested, tried, and imprisoned for "disseminating propaganda against the socialist regime." A number of Buddhist monks and Roman Catholic priests and lay workers had been placed under house arrest for "antisocialist activities." Amnesty International had released a report detailing how human rights violations were still common in Vietnam.

Hanoi surprises you from the very start by its lack of damage. There are a few girders missing from the middle spans of the Paul Doumer Bridge across the Red River, and from the window of the plane as you land at Noi Bia Airport you can see the water-filled remains of B-52 bomb craters, but otherwise the capital bears few scars of fifty years of almost continuous warfare.

Instead, Hanoi has miraculously—and somewhat paradoxically—survived as a time capsule of the French colonial era. It's no Paris, but the parks and boulevards of central Hanoi sustain an unequivocal French ambience. You see it in the effortless blend of natural and urban environments. You see it in the baguettes stacked on the back rack of a bicycle, in the old men in black berets playing cards in the parks, and in the old woman with the impeccable French accent who walks her Pomeranian around the Lake of the Restored Sword at dawn each morning.

But most of all you see it in the architecture, for many of the public buildings of Hanoi are colonial artifacts, planned and financed from Paris after the city was made the capital of the French Indochinese Union in 1902. The baroque-style Opera House is a mirror image of its Parisian prototype, and as if to accentuate the link, there was once a Café de la Paix just down the road. The Gothic proportions of Hanoi's Roman Catholic cathedral are a melodramatic contrast to the hodgepodge of dwellings that surround it, as if the whole neighborhood had been lifted en masse from a French country town. Art Nouveau is the predominant style of the Government Guest House, with dreamy wrought-iron fixtures, glass canopies, and a yellow-and-green motif similar to that of the older Metro stations in Paris. Nearly the entire diplomatic quarter is comprised of old French villas, the U.S. Consulate among them—a slightly dilapidated house at 19 Hai Ba Trung Street that waits for American diplomats to return.

Hanoi remains an urban anachronism because—unlike other colonial cities of Asia such as Singapore and Hong Kong—it has never had the economic impetus to knock down its architectural heritage in favor of high-rise. Even Communism cannot override the fiscal tenet that if you don't have money for new buildings the old ones will just have to do. But, by the turn of the century, assuming that the predicted economic boom takes shape, Hanoi *will* have skyscrapers. The question is one of preservation: how many of the colonial buildings will be spared demolition? Ask a dozen people, get a dozen answers. "I think we can't keep all the old houses, because some of them are built with bad materials," one lifelong resident of Hanoi told me. "But we don't want skyscrapers either. We were born on the earth and we should stay on the earth."

In Vietnamese, the Lake of the Restored Sword is called Hoan Kiem, a name also applied to the old district that surrounds it. This is the historical and spiritual heart of Hanoi. To the south and east of the lake is the French quarter with wide boulevards and grand villas; on the northern shore is the old Vietnamese quarter, a warren of narrow lanes and dark passages. In bygone times, each of the streets of the old town specialized in a specific product or service. The street names bear witness to this legacy: Hang Gai was the street of the hemp sellers, Hang Hom the street of coffin makers, Hang Bac the street of silversmiths, and so on. Although few of the original trades remain, the lanes still specialize, yet in far more modern merchandise. Hang Dau Street is illuminated each night with the naked bulbs of a dozen shoe stalls. Hang Dao is flanked by general clothing stores, where the young and restless of Hanoi buy their jeans and T-shirts. Hang Non is an open-air food market for the fresh produce of the Red River valley.

In French times, the old town was also a gathering place of intellectuals and subversives, one of the hotbeds of revolution. It was

Street scene in the old Hoan Kiem district of Hanoi. Vietnam's urban architecture draws inspiration from a number of sources, but the two primary influences are imperial Chinese and 19th-century French colonial design.

Hanoi has a surprising number of parks and gardens, leafy precincts that provide relief from the noise and claustrophobia or urban life. Here two men walk by a large banyan tree in the center of the business district of Hoan Kiem.

Tet Festival vignette in the Hai Ba Trung district of southern Hanoi. Kumquat trees are a favorite decoration for lunar new year.

Spinning "Van Phuc" silk at a factory in Ha Dong City on the outskirts of metropolitan Hanoi. The local silk industry has thrived in this town since at least the 11th century.

Some sidewalk smoke shops still provide bamboo pipes for the enjoyment of their older customers. Most of the younger generation prefer cigarettes, although foreign brands are now banned.

Last-minute purchase: a passenger buys limes from a vendor at Hanoi Station before departure of the daily train to Ho Chi Minh City in the south. The journey takes about 54 hours with stops in Vinh, Da Nang, Hue, and other coastal cities.

Capitalism and Communism clash on the streets of Hanoi: a street barber awaits customers near a mural extolling the virtues of socialist youth.

Entrance to an old shrine in the Hoan Kiem district of Hanoi. Notice the flying bat motifs above the archway and the procession of pilgrims on their way to a pagoda at top.

in a building at 48 Hang Ngang Street that Ho Chi Minh penned the Vietnamese declaration of independence. On Hang Dao Street was the Free School of Tong Kinh, a progressive nationalist group that (ironically) drew its inspiration from French political science and philosophy. The freethinkers have yet to return—at least in name—but the old town is once again the scene of lively discussion, the clamor of students, artists, government workers, and nascent businessmen who flock to a growing number of cafés and restaurants in the area, symbols of the grass-roots capitalism that is slowly creeping into the dark corners of this stodgy Communist city.

At a place called the Piano Bar, a tawny dog blends perfectly with the faded orange hue of the adjacent walls as he wanders between the tables in good French fashion. The waiters are young boys and girls, androgynous in their starched white shirts and little black bow ties. In one corner is a cabinet filled with what are obviously meant to be the good things in life: French cheese, brandy, an antique opium pipe, jade figurines, and silver bangles. There is a piano, of course, wedged against one wall of the dining room. Resting on top are a half-empty bottle of Johnny Walker and sheets of classical music. A young woman takes her place at a seat in front of the piano and is joined by a companion on violin, both of them students at the city conservatory. They play Mozart, then burst into a fractured version of "Waltzing Matilda" for the benefit of Australian friends.

By half-past nine, the place is nearly empty. The owner's wife slinks over to the piano, stunning in her green *ao dai*, a silk dress that covers her body from head to toe yet at the same time enhances her sinuous contours. The mood of the evening changes, as Mozart is put aside in favor of Vietnamese folk tunes that have the same haunting quality as the *chansons* of old Paris.

In another part of old Hanoi, a tiny café, nearly hidden from view by the gathering of bicycles parked outside, specializes in French coffee and yogurt made from fresh milk brought in each day from the countryside on the back of a bike. The proprietor is Hun Chi Le, typical of the thousands of Hanoi residents who have gone into business for themselves following the relaxation of legal restraints in the late 1980s. Le was born and raised in Hanoi, but in 1938 he was recruited by a French company to become a mechanic in New Caledonia. World War II intervened, and he didn't see Hanoi again until 1951.

"I was an automobile mechanic until three years ago, when I decided to open a café with my son and daughter," Le explained. "You must have a business license from the government, but there's

The streets of old Hanoi are alive with both people and products. There was a time when each lane had a separate function. Hang Ga was the street of the chicken sellers, Hang Hom the street of the barrel makers, Hang Muoi the street of the salt merchants, and so on. Other roads specialized in such diverse items as tobacco and opium pipes, lime and betel nut concoctions, paper offerings and coffins for the dead, river rafts and sails, silver jewelry and fermented fish.

OPPOSITE TOP: The French architecture of old Hanoi is characterized by a profusion of wooden window shutters, wrought iron balconies, ornate plaster cornices, red-tile roofs, and pastel hues. The overall effect can be distinctly Mediterranean.

OPPOSITE BOTTOM: Opened in 1911, the Opera House in Hanoi has survived the rigors of three different wars. Homesick Frenchmen flocked to this replica of the famous Paris Opera to see performances of ballet, classical music, comedy, and, of course, opera. In a further extension of the Paris metaphor, at one time there was even a Café de la Paix down the block where French colonials would gather afterward for a nightcap or game of cards.

no fee. It's really no problem. There are lots of small businesses now." Less than 20 percent of his profits go to tax. With the extra cash, he is slowly making improvements to the café: a new shelving unit here, linoleum panels over there. "But I'm not getting rich," he stated with a grin. "I'd like to go back to visit New Caledonia. But where can I get the three thousand dollars for the air fare? That's fifteen million *dong*! Impossible!" He paused a moment, rubbed the gray stubble on his chin, and continued. "Still, I have no desire to have many, many customers. Then this café would become impersonal. I like things the way they are now: I can talk to all of my customers. I know them all!"

If Hun Chi Le is indicative of Hanoi's grass-roots capitalism, then Nguyen Tran Bat is emblematic of how Western-style big business has also got its foot in the door. Bat is managing director of Investconsult, the first private limited company in Vietnam and one of just five firms licensed by the government as official investment consultants. Although its mandate covers all sorts of commerce, Investconsult is primarily in the business of exploiting the nation's vast mineral deposits by coupling foreign money and know-how with Vietnam's other great resource—unlimited labor.

I was introduced to Bat through a mutual friend, so our conversations were all the more absorbing because he wasn't urged upon me by the Foreign Ministry. Despite his title and position, Bat is one of the most unassuming businessmen I've had the pleasure to meet. Photos on his office wall testify to the fact that he can don jacket and tie when the situation dictates, but his preferred dress is jeans, leather sandals, and a loose cotton shirt. Brushing a thick wad of black hair from his eyes, Bat talked briefly about doing business in Vietnam. But he was quickly sidetracked onto other things: he wanted to teach me something of the substance of life in Hanoi, how the people live and what they think.

Bat thought it was critical that I understand the difference in mood between the north and south of Vietnam. "We in the north are like the sea. Sometimes we are the waves, sometimes we are the troughs. The north thinks about more than work. There is more balance in our life. The south is more dynamic in actions and appearance. But we in the north are more farsighted. The south is not the land where the nation was born. You might say it's like Texas when compared to New England. The southerners are more free with their gestures and the way they act. The northerners are quite different, not so outgoing. But these people are the origins of Vietnam. In order to

A statue of the Virgin Mary and Baby Jesus crowns a small park at the intersection of Nha Chung and Nha Tho streets in the old city. Behind looms the Gothic facade of Hanoi's Roman Catholic Cathedral, one of the most prominent relics of French days.

understand the Vietnamese character, you must come to the north, the real Vietnam."

Narrowing his focus to Hanoi, Bat explains how he is dismayed by the rapid growth in the city's population. It has doubled to nearly three million since the war, swollen by peasants who think they will find a better life in the big city, a rural conviction that isn't exclusive to Vietnam. At first the government espoused the theory that the state should build more factories in Hanoi to employ these people, but in recent years the city fathers have had a change of heart. "They don't want factories and all that pollution," says Bat. "People prefer light to dark."

Like many Vietnamese, especially those in the north who have been exposed to five decades of Marxist dogma, Bat expresses a profound indifference toward the whole concept of wealth. "We don't need a lot of money or material things," he claims. "We know how to arrange life with one dollar or with one million dollars. Even if you have one million dollars, you may not have a real girlfriend. But with one dollar you can find a very good woman." All very well and true. But statements like this are easy to make when you don't have money; they are much less common once the cash begins to flow, as in the south.

Still, I didn't doubt that Bat was sincere. He spent half an hour emphasizing the other foundations of life in Hanoi. Education was one. "We don't have many university graduates, but it's very difficult to find an illiterate person. People are very eager to learn. They read literature from many countries. They know very well the history of Great Britain, France, and America. They consider it a humiliation if no one is educated in a family."

Although he admits that very few people pray at temples nowadays, Bat is certain that Buddhism is still at the heart of society. "From a spiritual point of view, we rely on Buddhism. We believe there is a present life and a life after death. So we try to approach life with morality so that you never destroy your family."

Ah, the family. As in many Asian nations that is the apex of the social pyramid. "I may have a modern life, but I know how to balance and divide my money into three parts: one part for the family today, one part for the children in their future, and one part for me. The money for me, I can spend the way I like. But I never take money from the other parts and bring it to my part."

Bat talked about his family at length. His elderly mother was still alive. She could easily live off her son's income, a tidy little sum

Hanoi.

Quan Thanh Pagoda on the shores of West
Lake dates from the Ly dynasty era, nearly
a thousand years ago. It is dedicated to
Tran Vu, the God of the North, whose
spiritual attendants are a serpent and a tor-
toise. The French called this temple the
Pagoda of the Big Buddha.

A devotee places joss sticks in a niche at the Ha Pagoda as part of a festival in honor of the local gods.

Devotees burn paper offerings in a giant bronze caldron at Quan Su Pagoda during the annual Tet Festival, the lunar new year celebration. The shrine is also known as the Ambassador's Pagoda because it was originally built in the 15th century as a guest house for high-ranking Buddhist diplomats from around Asia. Since before the Second World War, Quan Su has been the fulcrum of Buddhist worship in the capital.

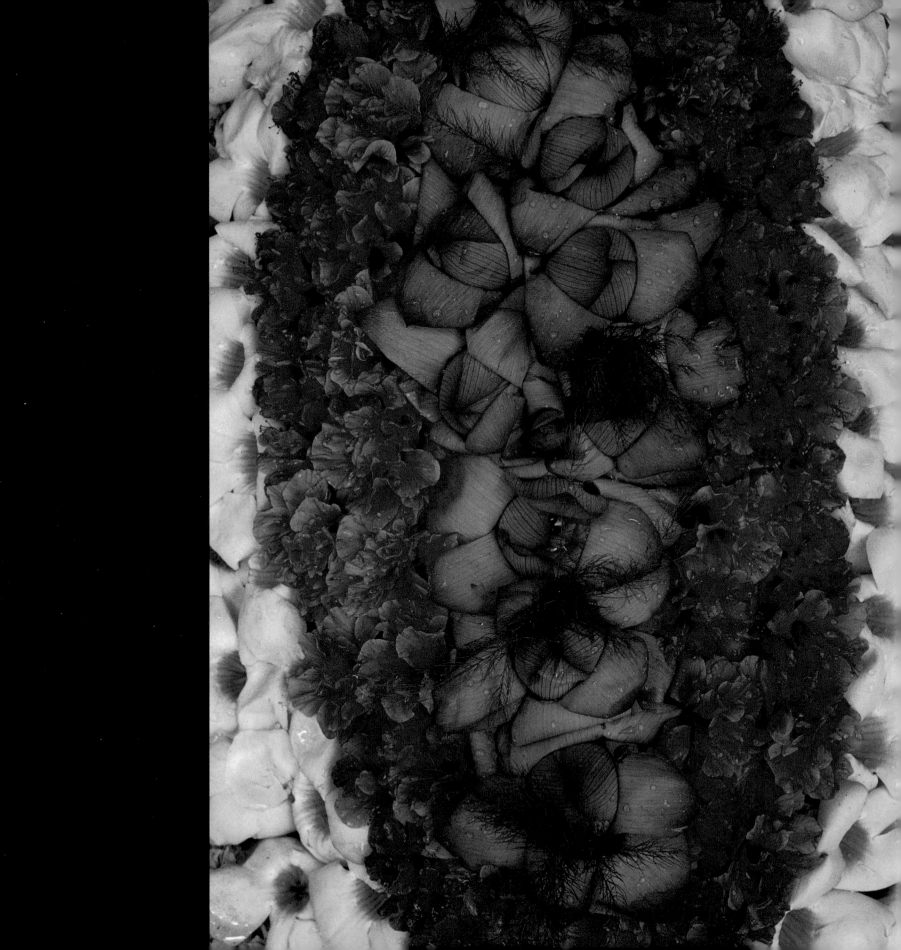

OPPOSITE: Funeral wreath in a flower shop in the Hoan Kiem district.

RIGHT: Freshly hewn gravestones stacked on the streets of the Hoan Kiem district.

BELOW: Mourners gather for a funeral in Hanoi. As in Western nations, flower wreaths are a common means to honor the dead.

A family mourns the death of a loved one in the Hanoi National Cemetery. The small boy at left holds a black-and-white photo of the departed. White rather than black is the color of death in most Buddhist cultures, hence the white headbands, veils, and, handkerchiefs made of mosquito netting.

by Hanoi standards. However, she insisted on running her own sidewalk stall, not so much for the money but for the social interaction. Bat's wife was an advice columnist for a local newspaper. "She counsels everyone but me," he laments.

Did she ever come across any wicked scandals? "Where you have humans you have social problems," he says philosophically. "But we don't have many in Hanoi. Just small ones. We have no gangsters or anything like that. Young people want to talk about the world outside; old people want to talk about the old times; middle-aged people want to talk about business." Bat finished with a message that I would hear throughout Vietnam: "We are indifferent about the war now. We don't want the same thing to take place. We don't want convulsions in our life. We want to arrange a separate circle in which we can be peaceful."

Like so many capital cities, Hanoi owes its existence to a strategic location on the banks of a great river, in this case the Song Hong or Red River, which emanates from the gnarled mountains of southern China as an offspring of Himalayan snow. At first the river is swift and narrow, passing through the narrow chasms of Yunnan and the northwest frontier of Vietnam. Yet by the time it reaches the vicinity of Hanoi, the Red River is fatigued and sluggish, ladened with orange-brown silt and interested in nothing more than finding the easiest path down to the Gulf of Tonkin. A thousand years ago, there was nothing but swamp, forest, and a few meager farms on the site of what is now Hanoi. Geopolitical considerations brought about a swift transformation.

About the time that Viking explorer Leif Eriksson reached America and the Normans were on the verge of conquering England, Vietnam was fractured into a feudal patchwork ruled over by autonomous warlords. This was the so-called Period of the Twelve Lords in the Red River valley. One of these rulers, Ly Thai To, eventually disposed of the others and founded the Ly dynasty. He established his capital on the southern bank of the Red River in the early eleventh century. The site offered a natural bastion against invaders and permitted easy access to the rich alluvial plains of the wide Red River valley. Thus, the new city could be easily defended and provisioned. The emperor called his new capital Thang Long (Ascending Dragon). Later known as Dong Do (Eastern Capital) and Dong Kinh (westernized as Tonkin), Thang Long would be renamed Hanoi (City between Two Rivers) in 1831.

Open markets in Hanoi are another hotbed of latent capitalism, in this case, the hundreds of fruit, vegetable, and meat dealers who gather each day to hawk the agricultural wealth of the Red River Valley.

Once the swamps were drained and dikes were built to protect against floods, Thang Long developed into a prosperous capital. A massive citadel and imperial palace complex rose on reclaimed land, while a thriving port evolved on the banks of the river itself in the area now called Hoan Kiem. Ships from all over the Orient and caravans from Central Asia came to hawk their wares here, as Thang Long grew into a thriving center of trade and commerce.

Court life in Thang Long was both rich and diversified. As early as 1042 laws were codified that set forth punishment for piracy and extortion, as well as prohibiting cruelty to farm animals and child slavery (although adult slavery was allowed). The emperor was personally responsible for overseeing the construction of dikes, and he encouraged the development of handicrafts both for royal demand and export. Ceramics, weaving, and metalwork prospered under the Ly regime, with a ready market in the imperial household.

As a patron of both the arts and intellect, the ruler also underwrote the cultural development of the city. The Temple of Literature was built at the southern gate of the city in 1070 as a seat of Confucian-learning. Several years later, the country's first university, Quoc Tu Giam, was founded as a training ground for mandarins who would become the civil servants of the realm. Various Buddhist pagodas in Thang Long also became seats of learning. Through such institutions, the Ly dynasty gave birth to Vietnam's first national literature, music, architecture, and decorative arts movements.

Thang Long was forced to weather a relentless stream of foreign invasions over the centuries. The Mongol hordes of Kublai Khan sacked the city on two occasions, although each time they were beaten back by Vietnamese counterattacks. But the powerful armies of Ming China held sway over the capital and the Red River valley for ten years before Le Loi's upstart victory in 1418, a battle that begot the legend of the Lake of the Restored Sword. Le Loi is said to have vanquished the Ming with a magical sword given him by a turtle in the lake. Another famous episode in the city's history took place in 1789, when Nguyen Hue, leader of the Tay Son revolt, staged a forty-day march on Thang Long to wrest the throne away from the corrupt Trinh emperor and preempt yet another Chinese invasion. In so doing, Nguyen Hue reunited Vietnam for the first time in two hundred years, but unwittingly paved the way for colonial occupation by giving his rivals an excuse to solicit French intervention. In 1883, the French gained control of the city, by now renamed Hanoi. It was the Red River that ultimately persuaded the French to choose Hanoi as

Street vendors in Hanoi tend to be a flexible lot. They can set up shop in a matter of minutes at just about any location: on sidewalks, in parks, and along the shores of the Lake of the Restored Sword.

Foreign consumer goods were relatively rare in Vietnam until the late 1980s, when economic reforms opened the door to both legal and black market imports. This street stall offers a wide array of exotic overseas fare: American soft drinks, Dutch beer, French champagne, and Russian vodka alongside the ubiquitous cans of local "333" beer.

Hanoi conjures stark images of a burned and bombed-out city. But in fact the city sustained little damage in World War II, the revolution against the French, or the American War. The vast bulk of central Hanoi is comprised of French colonial architecture in various states of repair, like this row of old shophouses in Hoan Kiem.

Fruit and vegetables for sale along the sidewalks of Hoan Kiem district in Hanoi.
Vietnamese cuisine has the same reliance
on fresh ingredients as other Oriental foods,
which means that produce must be trucked
from the countryside each morning.

their colonial capital: they saw the watercourse as a potential trade route into southern China.

Yet curiously—despite its cultural and historic associations—the people of Hanoi turn their back on the Red River today. There is no commercial interface with the water, no bustling docks or sweaty longshoremen as you would expect to find in a river city. That function was superseded by Haiphong during the French period. Neither are there lively markets or leafy parks along its banks. Rather, there are ugly earthen dikes that protect the city from floods. Pragmatism rules over pleasantries. "We don't think of the river in sacred terms, like people think of the Nile or the Tigris," Bat had told me. "We are more likely to think about the fact that it has good, fresh fish."

I will always remember the long summer nights in Hanoi. The days were miserable, far too hot and steamy for someone unacclimatized to spend outdoors. It wasn't until dusk that I dared to brave the streets. I walked for hours around the French quarter and the old town, watching the people and being watched in turn, a curiosity stimulated by exposure to unfamiliar cultures. It was a magical twilight, the sky an indigo blue, with flashes of lightning from the summer thunderstorms that appeared over Hanoi with an astounding regularity.

There were flashes of humanity too. A man toking on a bamboo pipe in the doorway of his shop. An old woman carefully brushing the hair of a doll, as if it were that of a human infant. Parents washing their child in a bucket at the side of the street. Teenage girls squatting on the pavement, selling fresh lychees, foreign cigarettes, and plastic AK-47 assault rifles. Above the counter in one shop is an old poster of Bruce Lee, all bulging muscles and glistening sweat. Farther along, a dozen kids sit mesmerized in front of a video screen. What are they watching? Bugs Bunny cartoons. Teenage girls scream and shout over a game of cards on the lawn next to the Lake of the Restored Sword. In the dark park beside the Opera House, young lovers smooch on the back of a scooter.

Hanoi has a stark deficiency of automobile traffic, simply the random olive-green jeep or black Volga sedan. Instead the streets are ruled by a chaotic alliance of pedestrians, bicycles, mopeds, and the three-wheeled *cyclos* that became an integral part of my Hanoi routine. The cyclo drivers who camped out in front of my hotel came to know me by name—although that didn't prevent them from trying to charge me five or six times the going rate for locals. One young driver was especially audacious, billing himself as "the number one cyclo driver in Hanoi." To prove it, he would pull out a pocketful of foreign business cards to show how many important people he had pedaled around town. I flipped through them one night: a New York psychiatrist who treated postcombat stress disorder; a child adoption expert from California; a registered nurse from the Women's Vietnam Memorial Committee. They were all Americans.

The lack of animosity toward Americans is bewildering. At the very least, I expected a few snide remarks or acerbic glances. After all, the Americans fought these people for more than ten years. Not only did they fight them in the jungles and tunnels of the south, but they bombed and strafed them in their own homes and schools in Hanoi. Surely, there must be some hard feelings. But if such angry emotions persist, they are kept well beneath the surface. From all evidence, the opposite is true: the people of Hanoi can't seem to get enough of Americans. They break into broad smiles at the discovery of a Yank. Young girls blush behind a hand-covered smile and teenage boys want to practice their English; the older people simply shake your hand.

The whole atmosphere of Hanoi seemed quite relaxed. Many of the rumors and innuendos I had heard in Bangkok appeared to be just that. No tension in the air. No acrimonious feelings. Instead, there was a pervasive grace despite the pressures and hardships that do exist behind the facade of everyday life. "It hasn't always been this way," said an Australian who has taught modern dance in Hanoi for three consecutive years. "When I first started coming here, people I worked with were afraid to invite me into their homes. You wouldn't believe how much things have loosened up in terms of personal freedom in just the last year."

At least at street level, personal freedom had expanded to the point where people were relaxed enough to engage in biting political satire in mixed company. An example of the prevailing humor:

Three ghosts were standing in a line to buy rice. One was fat, the second was thin and pale, while the third was a perfect physical specimen.
Two of them turn to the fat ghost and ask, "When did you die, that you're so fat?"
"I died in 1961," says the fat ghost. [The early 1960s are now considered the peak of Vietnam's economic development.]
The other two ask the good-looking ghost, "When did you die,

The Lake of the Restored Sword is a gathering place for many of the older residents of Hanoi, like this man who comes to meditate at this spot each morning at dawn. Others come to play cards, fish, or merely chat.

A boy snoozes on a bench in Indira Gandhi
Park, a small patch of green between the Hanoi
Town Hall and the Government Guest House.

During the hot and humid summer months, Hanoi exudes a relaxed tropical ambience. This resident has the right idea: reading a book in a hammock at Lenin Park.

Huc ("Sunrise") Bridge is often called the "Perch of the Morning Sun" because of its splendid views at dawn. It was built in 1855 to connect the eastern shore of the Lake of the Restored Sword with a small temple island. At the far end of the bridge is the thirty-foot-high Thap But ("Penbrush") Pagoda.

Fireworks explode over the Lake of the Restored Sword
on the eve of Tet, the last day of the old lunar year. Tet is
perhaps the most wondrous time of year in Vietnam, a
time of sumptuous banquets, pious temple visits, and joyous family reunions. Most business grinds to a halt two
weeks before Tet as people prepare for the celebration.

that you're in such good form?" "I died in 1972," he answers. [This was the last year of the American air raids, when Vietnam was at the crest of its international power.]
Finally they turn to the thin, pale one and say, "When did you die, that you look so miserable?"
"Oh, I'm not dead," he responds. "I'm still alive."

As the cultural heart and soul of Vietnam, Hanoi plays host to more than its fair share of creative bodies of one sort or another. Most of the professional guilds—cinema, drama, painting, dance, literature, and so on—are also based in the capital. These various cultural organs fall under the aegis of the ministries of Culture or Information, which means that, in effect, you produce culture and art for the bene-fit of the state, and you do so under the state's "benevolent" eyes.

Seven of the guilds are housed in the same building, the Literature and Arts Association on Trang Hung Dao. It was there that I went to meet one of Vietnam's prominent movie directors, Thanh An, who is also a standing deputy of the Vietnam Cinematography Association. I was ushered into a reception room on the second floor, cluttered with heavy-duty rosewood furniture, Ming reproductions, and Thai-style bronze buddhas. An assistant served tea and fresh lychees and placed a pack of Ruby Queen cigarettes on the wooden coffee table.

Thanh An surfaced a few minutes later. His appearance was strikingly eccentric for a Vietnamese, but in keeping with his role as a purveyor of the arts: jet-black hair that fell to his shoulders, pencil-thin mustache, silver-framed eyeglasses, and a white Panama-style hat tipped to one side of his head.

Like any good director, he provided the backdrop first. "Vietnam has a long culture, but in the last fifty years we've had much turmoil. So from an artistic point of view, we are very weak compared to your country. In the history of the world, few countries have suffered as much as Vietnam, or battled so long against so many invaders. So one of the most common themes in Vietnamese art is the woman waiting for her husband to come back from war. There are many stories about love—and suffering from love. Vietnamese people love, but not in a very strong way. They are a very balanced people."

With that out of the way, he launched into a vigorous personal history. Thanh is proud of the fact that he never went to cinematogra-phy school. He is self-taught, having learned on the job while making newsreels during the war. It wasn't until after 1975 that he started to direct feature films. "We don't have superstars, but we have actors

RIGHT: Miss Hanoi 1991: the first beauty queen to reign over the Vietnamese capital since before liberation. Here she is practicing the "vong" to keep her figure. An increasingly tolerant social climate has spurred the introduction of institutions that previously were taboo under the Communist regime.

BELOW: The Hanoi School of Dance carries on the fleet-footed traditions of both East and West, with a curriculum that ranges from classical European ballet to Vietnamese folk dancing.

who are good enough to make films," he explained. "Making films in Vietnam is very difficult; the demands are very high and the ability of the director is very limited. We can say that we want to do this or that, but we must change because it's not possible with our limited budgets or technical experience."

Thanh's films have twice been shown in the United States, at a festival sponsored by the East-West Institute in Hawaii and at an Asian film festival in New York City. He says that his most popular film is *Hanoi Girl*, but American audiences like *Dien Bien Phu Victory*. "The Americans told me that if they had seen this film before the war, they would never go to Vietnam," he laughed.

The Vietnamese get a few American films, especially those with a Vietnam War theme. *Platoon* is a mainstay of Vietnamese television, while *Born on the Fourth of July* is popular on the video circuit. In fact, for Thanh, Oliver Stone is something of a hero, the American who can do no wrong. "He has very generous eyes through which he sees the Vietnam War," said Thanh. "His films are very objective. We can understand the war and see the reasons for war. We see *Platoon* and we realized that Americans are not all bad-hearted. The Vietnamese people see these films and maybe meet one American soldier [veteran], and so they treat him like a friend."

Yet he spurns *Apocalypse Now* as mere exploitation. "I think it's terrible," Thanh moaned. "I will never forget one part of that film by Coppola where a helicopter starts bombing a Vietnamese village and the pilot likes very much to listen to Wagner. But with this music they show the destruction of the village. Yes, it was terrible."

Every year the Film Association churns out about twenty feature films, thirty documentaries, twenty animated productions, and seventy video short features. Many of the videos are shown on TV, although it's estimated that there are now some two hundred thousand VCRs in Vietnam. Very few films come up to export quality because of poor financing, bad technique, and shoddy materials. "We have to shoot on plastic film," he complained. "It's awful. Very bad quality. Because of Vietnam's hot climate, the color goes away very quickly. But it's cheap."

Thanh looks forward to the day when he can learn firsthand from Hollywood. "I have had a feeling for a long time that the American film family has sympathy with us and they support us. And I have a feeling in the future that we will have good cooperation. In the film profession, we need to learn from the Americans."

THE WARTIME CAPITAL

Boys will be boys, even in Vietnam. A group of local youngsters in blue jeans and baseball caps cavorts across old antiaircraft guns in Lenin Park in south Hanoi. The guns have been silent since 1973, but remain as a "playground" and reminder of the war.

OPPOSITE LEFT: At war for more than fifty years, Vietnam has more than its share of disabled veterans, like this visitor to Lenin Park who wears his old army helmet as a sign to all that he fought for his country.

OPPOSITE RIGHT: Soldiers of the 47th Regiment listen to their commanding officer read the newspaper while relaxing at their barracks in Hanoi. Despite the end of hostilities with the U.S. and China and the withdrawal of troops from Cambodia, Vietnam still keeps more than a million men in uniform, the world's fourth-largest fighting force.

As headquarters for the military high command that directed the operations of both the North Vietnamese Army (NVA) regulars and the South Vietnamese Communist guerrillas (Viet Cong), Hanoi was the nerve center of the Communist endeavor to topple the South Vietnamese government and drive the Americans from Indochina.

Despite its strategic importance, Hanoi suffered only minimal war damage, far less than London during the Battle of Britain. In theory, the U.S. Air Force and Navy were not allowed to bomb inside a ten-mile radius from central Hanoi. There were exceptions, of course, like the infamous "Christmas bombing" that destroyed much of the Kham Thien neighborhood in December 1972. But most of the American bombs were earmarked for suburban factories, the railroad yards on the north bank of the Red River, and the famous Paul Doumer Bridge. The bridge, a cantilevered steel span constructed by the French at the turn of the century, became a persistent symbol of North Vietnam's tenacious resistance to American force of arms. Despite repeated attempts and thousands of bombs (177 sorties), the Americans were not able to permanently sever the bridge. Workers quickly repaired it each time, keeping open the vital rail and road supply link to China.

American POWs—most of them pilots shot down on bombing raids over the north—were kept at various locations around Hanoi for the duration of the war. The most infamous compound was Hoa Lo Prison, dubbed the "Hanoi Hilton" by POWs. It was far from a resort. POWs were subjected to both physical and mental torture as their captors tried to force them to confess to war crimes. In keeping with the American GIs rather bleak sense of humor, individual parts of the prison were given nicknames. One notorious block was called the "Heartbreak Hotel"—solitary confinement where POWs were kept in tiny six-by-six foot cells. At the end of the war, the North Vietnamese released 558 American prisoners; many more are thought to have died during incarceration, although an exact figure has never been established.

Few other reminders of the war can be found in Hanoi, but you can make out "spider holes"—one-man sidewalk bomb shelters—by the light color of the cement that caps the holes. In the courtyard of the Army Museum are the rusting remains of U.S. planes shot down over the north. Surprisingly, there are few war monuments. One of the most poignant sits on the banks of West Lake, a remembrance of the antiaircraft gunners who protected Hanoi.

BLACK THAI AFFAIR

What is it about a nation's northwest frontier? Why are the inhabitants always so wild and woolly, remote from the firm control of central authority, beyond the sphere of heartland civilization? Pick from an assortment of nations—Canada, Pakistan, Brazil, Spain—and you find a northwest corner that is defiantly untamed, a place that revels in disparity.

Vietnam is no exception. Its northwest frontier provinces—collectively called the Northern Highlands—are far removed from Hanoi both in geography and in spirit. For centuries, rugged topography has prevented this region from integrating into the mainstream of Vietnamese civilization. Even today, this clenched fist of mountains and steep river valleys continues to defy the assault of lowland influences. Much of the highlands is inaccessible except on foot. In other places, roads and bridges have been washed away, or are in dire need of repair. Four-wheel drive is a prerequisite. It is possible to catch a plane into a couple of the mountain valleys—less than an hour from Hanoi as the crow flies—but the irregularity of flights, low clouds, poor visibility, and short runways turn this into a risky business.

This very isolation is what makes the highlands so fascinating from a human viewpoint. Ethnic Vietnamese don't predominate in this region as they do elsewhere in the country. In fact, outside of the market towns and provincial capitals, it's often difficult to find someone who even speaks Vietnamese. Instead, one finds a patchwork quilt of highland tribes. Black Thai and White Thai, Meo and Muong, and Hmong of three different shades. They have very little in common with the people of the flatlands. Rather, they look across the border for their cultural roots, to the hilltribe regions of Laos,

Her teeth stained with black lacquer as a sign of beauty, this woman has come to sell her vegetables at the daily market in Chieng Bac village, on the road between Son La and Dien Bien Phu.

Hanoi and vicinity.

Thailand, Burma, and southern China, the places where their ethnic cousins reside. In a larger sense, the northwest frontier is a place that has retained much of its cultural integrity, a part of Asia that remains "exotic" in the true sense of the word.

The uplands start just beyond Hoa Binh, a sprawling riverside town dominated by a massive Soviet hydroelectric scheme and the jumping-off point for Highway Six into the highlands. After engaging the services of a jeep and driver in Hanoi, I set out on a journey to a part of the northwest frontier that has been little explored by foreigners since the 1950s. Yet on this particular day it was impossible for me to behold the full scope of the mountains, as sheets of rain and heavy clouds obscured all but the lowest foothills. Still, there were unmistakable signs of a higher altitude: my breathing became labored as the air began to thin, and our engine groaned under the strain of numerous switchbacks.

Through the swirling mist the foothill farms brandished a faint Mediterranean mood, whitewashed walls with red-tiled roofs. These gradually gave way to homes with thatched roofs and wooden planks, an affirmation that we had crossed an imaginary boundary into hilltribe territory. This was also sugarcane country: dark maroon shafts with emerald foliage that matured to a height of more than twenty feet, soaring above the nearby tribal huts. The cane of this region is said to be especially sweet, eaten raw rather than refined, and sold as a treat in the markets of Hanoi.

It wasn't until we began to descend the precarious grade into the Mai Chau Valley that the rain ceased, the heavens cleared, and I got my first unobstructed view of the highland scenery. Flooded paddy fields glimmered like Inca silver, and sheer limestone knobs formed a crenellated barrier around the perimeter of the rice paddies, karst mountains that soared a thousand feet or more. It was like a pastoral scene in a Chinese painting: peasants and livestock trudging through the fields, with mist-shrouded peaks and twists of jungle as a backdrop. Somehow, I expected Chinese calligraphy to appear suddenly on the horizon, a short verse to complement the artist's brush.

Son La, an important market town and the capital of its eponymous province, has grown into a bustling little metropolis of more than a hundred thousand. And as a result of rapid growth in recent years,

White Hmong mother and child waiting for a bus on the road between Dien Bien Phu and Lai Chau. The Hmong are the eleventh-largest ethnic group in Vietnam, but a much larger number live across the nearby frontier in the rugged highlands of central Laos.

Much of the northwest frontier is studded with stark karst formations, like these sheer limestone knobs in the uplands of Ha Son Binh province.

OPPOSITE TOP: A tiny White Thai village sits like an island among paddy fields in the Mai Chau district. Muong longhouses tend to be larger and more elaborate than other hilltribe dwellings, with thatched roofs, bamboo floor, and planked walls set on stilts.

OPPOSITE BOTTOM: Muong on their way to market in the Lac Son district. The blouses of Muong women have V-shaped necks without silver buttons, the only visual cue that distinguishes them from the Black and White Thai.

RIGHT: The region around Man Doc village in Ha Son Binh province is renowned for its sugar cane. Much of the crop is trucked to Hanoi, where the cane is consumed in its raw state as a super-sweet snack. The cane grows to more than twenty feet, easily towering over the thatched dwellings of the local peasants.

OPPOSITE; CLOCKWISE FROM TOP LEFT:

The White Thai are considered the most fastidious of the hilltribe groups, as shown by the immaculate condition of this longhouse kitchen in the Mai Chau district.

A Muong woman toasting tea leaves at a commune in the Lac Son district of Ha Son Binh province. The official sources of income for this commune are tea and sugar cane, but bootleg liquor made from cane offers an alternative cash flow. There are also plans to reintroduce the cultivation of coffee, which the French once planted in this area.

Detail from the interior of a White Thai longhouse in the Mai Chau district of Ha Son Binh province. An empty beer can proves perfect as a joss stick holder. Fish tails, which are said to symbolize strength, bravery, and skill at hunting or fishing, are used to decorate the wooden beam.

The Lac Son area of Ha Son Binh province is home to nearly 100,000 members of the Muong ethnic group, a hilltribe with a language and customs similar to some of the indigenous tribes of the Philippines. This matriarch in Xua village smokes tobacco from a bamboo bong.

Black Thai girl hides behind her mother at the daily market in Chieng Bac, a thriving village astride the main road between Son La and Dien Bien Phu.

The headman's wife in Tong Nho village, a Black Thai settlement in central Son La province.

ABOVE: Lau flower quilts made at Van Ho commune in Son La.

Entrance to the notorious Son La Prison, where many Vietnamese freedom-fighters were held between 1908 and 1954. Most of the founders of the Communist revolution were interned here by the French; many of them died behind bars as a result of disease or torture. Solitary confinement was underground, so the cells could be flooded if prisoners got out of hand.

the town sports a perpetually unfinished air with roadworks and construction as the primary themes. Yet this flurry of activity obscures the fact that Son La is something of a warhorse, with a long and somewhat notorious history.

The ghosts of the highland past linger within the confines of the old French prison, perched on a bleak hill near the town center. Built just after the turn of the twentieth century, the prison was the scene of numerous guillotine executions, most of them of Black Thai warriors who resisted the imposition of French rule in their traditional homeland. Within its first ten years, the prison also witnessed at least one massive jailbreak and a Bastille-like storming of its bastions by Black Thai rebels who summarily dispatched the French commandant.

The most notorious phase of the prison's history began in the 1930s, when Son La became something of an inland Devil's Island for political prisoners from all around Vietnam. In a way, one established credibility as a Communist cadre by doing time at Son La, and most of the postindependence leaders of North Vietnam were imprisoned there at one time or another, including Le Duc To, Le Duan, and Truong Chinh. The most revered of the detainees was To Hieu, now elevated to a saintly position in the pantheon of early Communist leaders. To Hieu was allowed just fifteen minutes per day outside his tiny, windowless cell—during which he tended a small, flowering shrub that blooms to this day. But he also used this brief interlude to pass secret messages to other prisoners, notes by which he could communicate his political thoughts and organize a Communist cell within the prison. To Hieu died of pneumonia in 1944 during the Vichy French period, when the Japanese were in nominal control of Vietnam. Which is just as well, when you consider how the French hastened the end for other political prisoners.

Below the prison kitchen at the center of the quadrant were underground cells that could be flooded with water in a matter of minutes. This killing chamber was known only to local colonial authorities; it was kept secret from the French government in Paris and from inspectors dispatched to Son La in order to investigate alleged abnormalities at the prison. On May 13, 1941, French guards forced 156 prisoners into the underground cells and flooded them to chin level. Elbow-to-elbow, not able to sit or lie down, they were kept in water for nearly two weeks, all the while trying to stay awake, stay afloat, stay alive. Most of them didn't.

By the time we left Son La the weather had cleared, and while it was not quite sunny, I could already see the vast extent of the surrounding plateau. We climbed another steep grade, up to the Bon Phang region, where the landscape, fringed by villages with thatched-roof homes, was a golden brown, the rice ready for harvest. Hundreds of people hiked along the highway, commuting to the local market in Bon Phang village, where we found an itinerant magician entertaining hundreds of people in the town square. Most all of them were Black Thai, distant kin to the people of Thailand and among the most prosperous of the highland tribes, whose wealth is based on rice and the other things they grow. Taking advantage of the rich soil, they display great ingenuity in the various mechanical contraptions traditionally used to transport water from stream to field.

Like many mountain tribes, the Black Thai tend to wear their wealth. This is especially true of the women, with their silver buttons and bangles and elaborately decorated costumes. For most hilltribe sobriquets, the color reference is to the primary hue of the women's skirts, in this case a smooth raven-colored wrapping that drops to their ankles. Above the waist, the Black Thai ladies adorn themselves in brilliant blouses in shades of pink and lavender and aquamarine, with big silver buttons in the shape of butterflies. They wear their hair in a bun, concealed by a black scarf bordered in the intricate embroidery for which the Southeast Asian hilltribes are justly famous. The men still prefer basic black pajamas, often with oblong wooden buttons. Their one nod to fashion is the French beret, popular in the highlands for more than fifty years.

Turning northwest of Tuan Giao and traversing a narrow pass that leads to Dien Bien Phu, we noticed dozens of Black Thai panning for gold in a stream adjacent to the road. It was an unusual process, an assembly line of five or six people on each team. Upstream, a muscular man guided a metal sled along the bottom with the aid of a bamboo pole. Meanwhile, two women pulled the sled from the other end using ropes attached to a simple wooden capstan. A third woman shoveled silt from the sled onto a wooden washboard, where another man—the actual panner—washed it down with water in a meticulous search for gold. It was arduous work, yet the miners told me that it was worth every ounce of sweat, much better than laboring in the paddy fields. Their average daily find was about a tenth of an ounce, which they could sell for

This may resemble a rafting contest, but these Black Thai are really panning for gold in a stream between Tuan Giao and Dien Bien Phu. The daily take is about a tenth of an ounce, which fetches $40 from assayers in Hanoi, which is far better than what these people could earn tending crops.

270,000 dong ($40) to local assayers or in the gold shops of Hanoi. That was a hefty salary for these parts, even if it was split five ways.

Despite their somewhat primitive technique, the goldminers are unconscious prophets of the highland future. Foreign firms already are scrambling for the rights to exploit the vast mineral wealth known to lie beneath the ground. Once the bulldozers and earthmovers go to work, no one will be able to stop the highlands and its people from changing overnight.

"The northwest is loaded with minerals," Kevin Edwards had told me back in Hanoi. A phosphate expert who once ran the Australian mining operation on Christmas Island in the Indian Ocean, Edwards was in Vietnam as a consultant to a private investment firm that wanted to get in on the ground floor of the mining bonanza. "Oil, natural gas, copper, bauxite, phosphate, gold, rare earths, and massive coal reserves—you name it," Edwards continued. Among other "strategic minerals" known to exist in the northwest region are tin, lead, tungsten, silver, and zinc. Rare earths include columbium, barite, fluorite, strontium, tantalum, thorium, and uranium. The list goes on and on, almost every precious metal known to man.

To exploit these vast mineral reserves, the Hanoi government is contemplating the renovation of the old narrow-gauge railway line through the Red River Gorge. Roads are being punched into isolated parts of the mountains, and eventually airfields will be constructed or upgraded to ferry in mining engineers like Edwards. He walked over to a map on the office wall and stabbed his finger at a yellow sector. "Hoang Lien Son province. Packed full of minerals. Very rich area." I could see the glint in his eyes, the same fever that had taken men to California, Kalgoorlie, and the Klondike a century earlier. Now the first of the high-tech prospectors were pounding at the door of Vietnam.

Dien Bien Phu holds a special place in the French psyche, in the same compartment with memories of Waterloo and Agincourt. The very name is emblematic of defeat and surrender. The Battle of Dien Bien Phu in 1954 not only spelled the end of French dominion in Indochina, it also marked the end of France as a great world power. After this, the colonies started to peel away one by one, until there was merely a skeleton of the once-extensive French Empire. The battle also marked the triumph of Ho Chi Minh and Communism in Vietnam, the beginning of a multifarious political and diplomatic campaign that would eventually draw Americans into war in Indochina.

But that was long ago, a different era, before most of today's Vietnamese were born. The tanks and mortars have given way to the spade and plow. Nowadays, Dien Bien Phu is just another mountain valley where people' get on with the future rather than dwell on the past. Hill A1 has been transformed into a monument to the Vietnamese victory, ignored by the townspeople and locked away behind metal gates and barbed wire. The adjacent cemetery is equally forsaken. "Of course, it has only Vietnamese," said my local guide.

OPPOSITE LEFT: A ninety-eight-year-old resident of Sum Mun village, a Black Thai community in the Dien Bien Phu valley. She claims her village hasn't changed a bit since she was a child in the 1890s: there still isn't electricity or running water. Her only complaint: "I have a sore back!"

OPPOSITE RIGHT: Mother and infant at Phu village in the Dien Bien Phu valley. The settlement has about 600 people, nearly twice as many as a generation ago because of the high birth rate. Most parents boast five or six kids; contraceptives are virtually unheard of. The people make their living from harvesting rice and the production of raw silk.

RIGHT: Making baskets and brooms from bamboo in the municipal market at Dien Bien Phu.

"The French took their dead home." The Dien Bien Phu Museum was open, but also empty. The only thing that seemed to linger is a deep-seated hatred for the French, the fallout from their brief but brutal reign of terror in this valley.

Like much of the rest of Vietnam, the valley of Dien Bien Phu has a long history of struggles against foreign oppressors. At one time or another it has shouldered invasions from Thailand, Laos, and China. There was aggression from the Red River valley, too, but no one talks about that these days. All you hear are half-hearted diatribes about the solidarity of the Vietnamese and their poor hilltribe cousins. But it doesn't take much to imagine that the Black Thai and other mountain peoples fought with as much tenacity against the Vietnamese as they did everyone else. If this were just another mountain valley, it would never have attracted so many aspiring conquistadors. But for centuries, Dien Bien Phu was a central node in the lucrative caravan network that linked Thailand, southern China, and the Red River valley, a sort of miniature Samarkand of the hills. Its strategic and economic value was beyond reproach. "Trade was booming," Nguyen Van Sy, a member of the district committee, told me. "This valley was very crowded at that time. They traded silver, clothes, agricultural and forest products. They mined silver in this area. And they grew opium too!"

Such wealth was bound to draw the attention of scoundrels, like the ruthless Laotians who marched over the mountains in the mid-eighteenth century. In a move to intimidate the people of the valley and suppress any thoughts of dissent, they rounded up hundreds of children and took them to an isolated spot where they drowned them all. Their bleached bones were shown to the grieving parents, but they were powerless to oust the invaders. This is when General Hoang Cong Chat, a shrewd military mind, was sent up from Hanoi—not so much to conquer the valley but to make sure that no other great power of Southeast Asia did so. He whipped the Black Thai into a deadly fighting force. It took a year, but they succeeded in driving the Laotians from the valley.

The final victory was in 1758 (what the locals like to call the First Battle of Dien Bien Phu) and, through an ingenious strategy called the "Goat Defense," it was won without a drop of blood being spilled. It was really quite simple. Hoang Cong Chat had gathered three hundred goats under cover of darkness and hidden them in the hills. One evening lighted candles were fixed to the goats' horns, and the animals were herded down a mountain pass in full view of the Laotian camp. As was intended, the enemy looked up, saw this mass of quivering light, and presumed that it was massive reinforcements arriving from Hanoi. The Laotians fled in panic, never to return.

Hoang Cong Chat lived in Dien Bien Phu for ten years, until his death in 1768. During that time he constructed a citadel at the center of the valley to guard against future invasions. The remains of the citadel still can be seen today, crumbling ramparts and moats that form the confines of a Black Thai village called Phu. The general's grave lies next to a tranquil pond, and a simple adobe shrine has been built on the site. Offerings of bananas, limes, and sesame cakes sit on the mud doorstep, while inside, above the altar, is a portrait of the general on a white steed.

We spent several days exploring the valleys to the north of Dien Bien Phu, one of the most isolated and primitive parts of Vietnam. A foray into this area presents several hazards, not the least of which is the appalling condition of the roads. Whole parts of the roadway had crumbled a thousand feet down the side of mountains, and some of the routes disintegrated into slimy tracks with mud a yard deep in places. But our jeep did the job, with four flat tires and a broken tailpipe to show for the effort.

As if the roads themselves weren't hazard enough, the region between Dien Bien Phu and Lai Chau is also the realm of bandits— army deserters who fled into the mountains. Desertions have become such a grievous problem that the Vietnamese Army trains young recruits inside a cordon of barbed wire and armed guards. Those who succeed in escaping to the northwest frontier face little danger of being caught. More than police or army, their most deadly enemies are cold and starvation. The deserters prey on passing motorists out of desperation. I knew it was true: the last Western journalist who passed this way was accosted at gunpoint and had his camera stolen.

Yet the risks are worth the rewards, an opportunity to study an astounding array of ethnic groups that harks back to a distant time when the entire earth was populated by small rival tribes. In one valley alone there were five different groups, each living in a separate village and speaking its own unique tongue.

At times it's "hard to tell the players without a card," as the old

American baseball saying goes. Separating the Thai from the Hmong is easy enough, but identifying the various sub-groups within these tribes is a bit like trying to differentiate between navy blue and black in a dimly lit room. You quickly learn a few tricks of the ethnologist's trade. One of the most important clues is the pattern of a woman's blouse. Black Thai women sport a round collar that fits tightly around the neck; White Thai ladies prefer a V-shaped neck; Muong women also have V-shaped neck but with a small slit that runs down to the first button. With the various Hmong clans the challenge is stiffer. There are four groups along the northwest frontier, with names based on the color or pattern of the women's skirts: Black, Red, White, and Flowered. However, nowadays the groups tend to mix and match these motifs. For instance, on the banks of the Nam Muc River, I met a group of hilltribe people waiting for a country bus, White Hmong but wearing blue denim "travel" skirts.

Matters are even more complex if you consider that the Hmong are also called by their old name, the Meo. It seems the central government rechristened these people in order to terminate a social stigma that had long been attached to the Meo. My guide explained the background: "The Meo were always considered a dirty, unhygienic people who rarely bathed and who smelled. They looked dirty, and no one wanted to go near them." The authorities in Hanoi concluded that by changing the tribal name, people would be more likely to embrace the Hmong/Meo and bring them into the fold of mainstream society.

But this sort of misguided bureaucratic reasoning failed to address the fact that the social fabric of these mountains is based on a crude caste system. The White Thai are at the peak of this pyramid, considered the most modern and wealthy of the minority groups. The Black Thai are a notch below. There is little intermarriage between these tribes, but in such cases the Black always goes to live in the White village out of deference to their higher standing. Both of the Thai groups live in valley bottoms and are wet rice farmers. That puts both groups a notch above the Hmong, who cultivate dry rice on inferior plots on the slopes. A Thai would never think of marrying a Hmong. That would be the ultimate social disgrace. More than any other factor, ancient customs such as these have preserved the distinctions among the mountain peoples, even those living adjacent to one another.

While the hilltribes hold out against one another, they are grad-

Black Thai women are known for their silver. It can often cost up to 200,000 dong ($40) to purchase the raw silver that goes into forging the butterfly buttons on the blouse. The coin in her hair is a twenty-cent piece from French Indochina circa 1930, although old silver coins from Thailand are also favored.

OVERLEAF:

LEFT: Woman of the Red Hmong clan harvesting dry rice on a farm between Dien Bien Phu and Lai Chau. The Hmong are among the poorest of the hilltribe people, with little access to modern health or education facilities. They scrape a meager living off the land, growing rice, maize, and vegetables, and raising chickens, pigs, and ponies.

RIGHT: The Hmong are divided into four separate tribes named after the predominant design motif of the women's dress: Black, White, Red, and Flower clans. These particular girls are Red Hmong who inhabit the isolated Sin Chai Plateau in eastern Lai Chau province.

ually and almost imperceptibly drawn into the pervasive Viet culture. Some of it is voluntary, that worldwide phenomenon of tribal people coming into contact with modern civilization and deciding they would rather wear a pair of cheap jeans than their traditional garb. But it's also government policy. Minority languages are not taught in district schools; it's up to the parents to coach their kids in Thai or Hmong speech and writing. It was the same story in every village: the vast majority of children were illiterate in their native tongue; only about half could speak it. Within a generation, the hilltribe languages might be extinct except among the elderly.

In the Lai Chau Valley, I talked with White Thais who have already cast off their traditional language and dress and are now in the process of abolishing their traditional architecture as well. Thatched roofs are being replaced by slate tiles; wood or bamboo walls are making way for adobe. The root cause isn't so much state policy as it is environmental mismanagement by both the tribes and the central government. "Thatch is getting harder to find," said one villager, busy cutting slate tiles. "Too many people have gathered it from the hills over the years and brought it home. We had to find another roofing material. It's much easier to get slate. Forest products like timber are also harder and harder to find." To confirm his words, all I had to do was gaze at the deforested slopes behind his village.

Yet for now, ancient ways still persist in much of the highlands. The farther you get away from the major roads the more modern influence wanes. One such place is the Nguyen Sin Chai Plateau, a region where life is caught in something of a time warp. The route up from Lai Chau was long and treacherous, most of it along the edge of a sheer vertical drop. We cleared a final pass and advanced into a magical landscape, a mixture of forest and glade strikingly similar to the Highlands of Scotland. The people of the plateau were unlike any hilltribe group we had seen before. We stopped to talk to a couple of girls collecting water at a stream, but they ran away in fright at the sight of a white face. A bit farther along, we spied an older woman with two children, but they too fled into the bush before we could learn their origin. It was another half hour before we came across a pair of men in black pajamas who identified themselves as Black Hmong, one of the most shy and primitive of the minority groups in Vietnam. They have lived in these mountains for centuries, all the while giving wide berth to strangers. This pair was headed for a White Thai village in the valley below, where they would barter a pair of chickens in bamboo cages for batteries. "We get six batteries for one chicken," they told us, all excited.

Later, along the same road, we saw a dozen men with guns and assumed they were bandits. They moved swiftly through the landscape as if pursuing something, intersecting the highway just ahead of our jeep. At such a time your heartbeat quickens and your mind races with thoughts of how to handle the impending confrontation. But this time it was a false alarm: no more than Black Hmong stalking wild boar with primitive flintlock rifles and hunting dogs.

Down in the valley of the Nam Muc River, one of our most interesting finds, along the side of the road, was a burial site, the grave of a young White Thai woman who had died from natural causes just a few days before. It was a rare glimpse into the ancient religious customs of an animistic tribe numbering no more than two hundred thousand adherents in the northern highlands of Vietnam. Towering above the grave was a bamboo scaffold, perhaps forty feet high, and suspended from this were the dead woman's clothes. Over the grave itself was a tiny wooden house with a thatched roof, a scale model of the typical White Thai dwelling. Inside were placed various items the deceased would need in the afterlife: bits of food, a

Colorful streamers and the clothes of the deceased adorn a White Thai burial site at Pa Ham village in Lai Chau Province. The grave is that of a twenty-four-year-old woman who had died four days earlier. Her body rests in the elevated "grave house" at left, which also contains items she will need in the afterlife: mosquito net, quilt, floor mat, and a tiny round chair for her ghost to sit on.

A page from the Black Thai "almanac" that governs much of the spiritual and corporal life of Tong Nho village. This particular segment is part of the annual horoscope, showing the months June through December. The horizontal humans and upturned livestock represent death: bad months in which to sow crops, build a house, or start a family.

About 270 White Thais live in Lat village in the Lai Chau district. The standard of living here is much higher than other villages in the valley because of alluvial gold found in the nearby stream. The inhabitants also grow rice and raise livestock for sale in the local market.

mosquito net, a thick quilt, a floor mat to sleep on, and a little wooden stool on which to sit. The roof was shrouded in a black and red quilt with tiny embroidered flowers, and the house was surrounded by yellow, pink, and green streamers fixed to bamboo poles. Burning joss sticks were planted in the soil at the head of the grave, adjacent to which was a small wooden altar with animal bones and cow horns.

In Tong Nho, a Black Thai village in the Son La district. Tuang Van Mang, the eighty-five-year-old village elder, produced a dusty leather valise and dug deep inside, extracting a book wrapped in plastic to protect it from the elements. "This is the Black Thai almanac," said the old man. "It goes back four or five generations in my family." Inside were colorful zodiac charts, various numerical tables, and other means by which Tuang guided the everyday life of Tong Nho village.

Tuang flipped through the almanac, explaining the significance of each page. "It has illustrations to determine the good and bad days to start building a new house, get married, plant crops, and so on, and it contains personal fortune charts. Everything is determined by sixty-day cycles that are repeated six times each lunar year. The book also has instructions on how to position the house. If the door is fac-

Laden with Chinese consumer goods, Vietnamese stream back across the border at Dong Dang in Lang Son province. Although the frontier is officially closed, grassroots trade is tolerated by officials on both sides of the border.

OVERLEAF:

LEFT: A traditional Vietnamese junk plies Hailong Bay on the northeast coast. The long bamboo poles support small drift nets.

RIGHT: Hailong Bay has long been considered one of Vietnam's premier beauty spots. Jagged karst formations rise hundreds of feet from the deep blue waters of the bay, creating countless caves and channels that are best explored by boat. According to local legend, the rugged topography was created by a huge dragon trying to make his way from the highlands to the sea.

ing the dragon's head—as in this illustration—then the inhabitants will be gobbled up. Doors should always face the dragon's body. We still use this book now. The villages always ask my advice for new houses, wedding parties, and so on."

As headman, Tuang was also the village shaman. Using the almanac as his celestial guide, he practiced astrology and told fortunes and visited sick people in their homes. "Becoming the headman doesn't depend on your wealth or your family," he explained to me, using his eldest son as a translator. "It depends on your knowledge. Before, in the old days, people who had good knowledge of these matters set up a school for others to learn. But not anymore." I asked what would happen to the book and its store of knowledge after his death. "If I die, anyone in my family who wants to learn or view this book can do so. It depends on the children—if they want to or not. Someone from the village will be trained to read this book, to be my successor."

Whether the Black Thai almanac or other vestiges of hilltribe culture survive into the next century is anyone's guess. No one would want to deny them progress, or a better standard of living. But there seemed to be a misplaced assumption among the powers that be in Vietnam that, as in other countries, progress can only be gained by cleansing the tribes of their traditional culture. As I left the highlands, heading back for Hanoi, the thought struck me that I was watching the last stand of a vanishing way of life.

DIEN BIEN PHU

The culmination of eight years of brutal colonial war between the French and the Vietnamese came between March and May 1954. Weary from the hit-and-run guerrilla tactics favored by the Viet Minh—a coalition of Vietnamese Communists and nationalists—the French tried to force the enemy into a set-piece battle where they would have the upper hand with superior firepower. At the same time, Paris hoped that a stunning victory over the Viet Minh would strengthen their hand at the upcoming peace talks in Geneva. The French high command, under General Henri-Eugène Navarre, chose Dien Bien Phu to make their stand.

From the very start of the operation, the French both overestimated their own ability to wage a mountain campaign and underestimated the Viet Minh's aptitude as a military force. Navarre committed sixteen thousand paratroops to the cause, including members of the elite French Foreign Legion, who parachuted into the valley at the end of 1953. The French strategy was clear: draw the Viet Minh into battle and then trap them in a pincer of reinforcements moving up from the rear. The French were confident that the fortifications of Dien Bien Phu were impregnable to attack by a peasant army.

In response, the Viet Minh surrounded the valley with sixty thousand troops. General Vo Nguyen Giap—later a hero of the American War—planned the attack, which is now con-sidered a masterpiece of military tactics. His ace in the hole was artillery, taken apart and carried over the mountains, where it was reassembled and dug into the slopes facing Dien Bien Phu.

Battle commenced on March 13 with a massive artillery bombardment of French positions at Him Lam, Ban Keo, and Doc Lap. Next came cleverly staged infantry attacks. Flanks of the French fortifications collapsed, but Hill A1 and the rest of the center held tight. Dien Bien Phu settled into a two-month battle of attrition. Almost at once the French were cut off from their nearest supply base 180 miles away—and made to rely on a risky airlift of food and ammunition. The French reinforcements that were supposed to move in from the rear were never able to fight their way through the mountains. In desperation, Paris asked both London and Washington for aerial support, but the request fell on deaf ears. For their part, the Americans saw the French decline as their own window of opportunity into Southeast Asia.

The final assault came on May 7, as another human wave overwhelmed the last French defenses. Colonel De Castries surrendered with ten thousand troops, and the hundred-year-long French stranglehold on Indochina effectively came to an end.

CRADLE OF

REVOLUTION

We left Hanoi before dawn, heading south out of the city and into the wide-open plains of the Red River valley. Within fifteen minutes we were in the countryside. A white mist hung low over the palms and paddies, adding a romantic aura to the land. The rich aroma of cooking fires blended with the typical smells of the barnyard, the trademark fragrance of a fertile land.

The road ran straight and narrow, sticking close to the course of the old French railway that also terminates in the deep south. A steam train came lumbering in the opposite direction, belching black smoke and straining under the weight of dozens of boxcars. In front of mud-brick and thatched-roof houses, peasants performed their morning *tai chi,* and there was a young woman in white pajamas combing long, silken hair that reached down below her waist.

Water was pervasive, the ultimate giver of life, and each body of liquid was a drama unto itself. An elderly man with a gray goatee fished from inside a bathtub-sized craft in a murky pond. Stout wooden boats with lateen sails headed upriver against the wind. Dozens of buffalo lounged in the middle of a canal with just their heads protruding above the surface, and nearby men cast nets or tended to bamboo fish traps. Peasants were up to their elbows and knees planting emerald green rice stalks, while others scooped even more water into the paddies with the aid of a wicker basket attached to a primitive swinglike apparatus that lifted the liquid up and over the dikes.

The sun rose as a giant blazing ball over the Tonkin Gulf, and for the first time I could discern the extent of the plains. The vast expanse of Vietnam spread before me.

Water buffalo lounge in a stream between Quang Tri and Hue. The ancient road through this region was called the Route of the Mandarins. The French called it the Street Without Joy because of bloody fighting during the Vietnamese war of liberation. Today it's merely Highway One, the major route between north and south.

OPPOSITE: The Red River valley is one of the most fertile regions of Asia, but farming methods, including irrigation, have changed little over the last thousand years. Humans and animals still do most of the work, toiling in the fields from sunrise to sundown, seven days a week.

Freshly painted paper banners dry in the sun in anticipation of a local festival at Dong Ho village in Ha Bac province.

More than eighteen million people crowd into the cities, towns, and hamlets of the Red River valley. This is the heartland of a nation, a place as vital to the birth of Vietnamese civilization as the River Nile to ancient Egypt or the Indus to early Indian culture. It was here that humanity first took root, and where it matured into an advanced society.

Stone Age man lived in limestone caves around the periphery of the valley, taking advantage of the natural abundance of the land. With the advent of rice culture about six thousand years ago, man moved down to the marshy flatlands and established an agrarian society now called the Lac Viet culture. Although its origins are obscured in myth and legend, the first dynasty was a confederation of fifteen clans ruled by a line of eighteen Hung kings from a village capital near present-day Hanoi. Their successors, the Au Lac kings, were inundated by immigrants from southern China in the third century B.C., the start of more than a thousand years of Chinese dominance in the Red River valley.

It wasn't until A.D. 939—after the battle of Bach Dang—that the Vietnamese regained independence from China. The victors established their capital in the heart of the Red River valley, as did five subsequent dynasties that are collectively responsible for the creation of Vietnamese culture as we know it today.

Few traces of these civilizations remain—ruins here and there, a few crumbling temples. But their glory lives on in the festivals of the region, celebrations that trace their origins to dynastic times, rites that have endured despite the intrusion of modern warfare and Communism.

A festival takes place each year among the ruins of the earthen citadel at Co Loa, capital of the Au Lac kingdom, now set amid rice paddies just north of Hanoi. A procession celebrates the legend of An Duong, the last king of the dynasty, and his evil daughter Mi Chau, who betrayed the secrets of the kingdom to Chinese invaders. Some ancient rituals are more religious in nature, like the spring pilgrimage to Huong Pagoda in Ha Son Binh province. Thousands of Buddhist devotees make the trek on foot or by water in small boats along the Yen River, visiting sacred caves and temples along the way. Other celebrations are rooted in peasant life, like the Hoi Lim Festival in Ha Bac province, a melodic singing competition between boys and girls from the same village.

A vendor sells an assortment of fireworks at his shop in Hanoi prior to the Tet Festival.

LEFT: The temple festival at Co Loa takes place on the sixth day of the first lunar month, amid the ruins of an ancient city on the Red River plains north of Hanoi. Co Loa was the capital of Vietnam more than two thousand years ago, at the end of the Bronze Age. The most popular monarch of that period was King An Duong who was betrayed by his daughter in a battle with invading Chinese. Ironically, both father and daughter are revered at the annual festival.

OPPOSITE:

TOP LEFT: This boy works 24 hours a day for two weeks before the Tet Festival to make lotus seed candy, a favorite at the Tet festivities.

TOP RIGHT: Residents mob shops and street stalls in the center of Hanoi in the last days before Tet. Traditional new year decorations include flowers, peach blossoms, and miniature kumquat trees.

BOTTOM LEFT AND RIGHT: Firecrackers, joss sticks, and other combustibles are sold at shops all around Hanoi in the run up to the Tet Festival.

THIS PAGE:

ABOVE LEFT: Wrestling and other games are a big part of the Hoi Lim Festival.

ABOVE RIGHT: Giant chess game underway at the Hoi Lim Festival in Ha Bac province on the northern fringe of the Red River valley. The festival takes place two weeks after Tet, the lunar new year.

RIGHT: The primary attraction of the Hoi Lim Festival is the song contest, in which teams of men and women compete against each other in courtship tunes. The melodies have remained the same for hundreds of years, but the lyrics are improvised to reflect contemporary themes and current events.

The Firecracker Festival resonates through Dong Ky village in Ha Bac province two weeks after lunar new year. Local families compete to see who can build the biggest and best fireworks, and the climax of festivities is the ignition of these explosive contraptions in a field outside the village. Injuries are common and deaths sometimes occur, but that doesn't dissuade spectators from crowding as close to the violent action as possible.

The sixteen clans of Dong Ky village spend the entire year making their elaborate firecracker displays, often spending in excess of $500 on explosives and decorations. The combustive "floats" are paraded through the streets, blessed by the village elders, and then everything goes up in smoke until next year.

But the most auspicious and most anticipated celebration is Tet, the lunar new year, a time of wild and wondrous things in the Red River valley. Tet commemorates the end of winter and the start of spring, traditionally a time to replant crops. Yet before the work begins, a great festival ensues. Work and school grind to a halt all over the north, as families prepare for the most joyous time of the year. Mother and daughter are hard at work preparing special delights like lotus-seed candy and bean cakes, or purchasing miniature kumquat and peach trees at the local market. Father is at the family shop, clinching last-minute deals and balancing the books so he can start the New Year with a clean slate. Son is setting off firecrackers behind the house with other village boys. The action reaches a climax on the eve before Tet, as the entire village gathers to watch a fireworks display over the duck pond. The actual day of Tet is blatantly quiet, set aside for family visitations and prayer at the local pagoda, an indelible link with the past.

The end of Tet means hard work for peasants in the Red River valley, unenviable chores that are necessary to coax life from the soil: toiling behind the buttocks of a huge water buffalo while guiding the animal and its plow across a muddy field; bending over for hours,

ABOVE: Silent, solitary prayer at the Ha Tri Pagoda outside Hanoi in Ha Son Binh province.

TOP RIGHT: This ancient tea ceremony is re-enacted at a local village festival.

CENTER AND BOTTOM RIGHT: Like most Vietnamese shrines, Den Ba Chua Kho Temple in Ha Bac province stages an annual celebration to honor local gods. Burning joss sticks and food are offered to the temple deities in return for prosperity and good fortune over the coming year.

replanting bright-green rice stalks, and then later harvesting the crop; stacking the grain in the back of a bullock cart, then spreading the rice out to dry in the village square or along the nearby highway; and finally, husking the rice before it goes to market. This perpetual cycle of life has outlasted every dynasty, as surely as it will survive any political system.

It was near Hoa Lu, the first capital of an independent Vietnam after the Chinese occupation, that we came across a peasant by the name of Van. When she wasn't tilling the fields, Van made extra money rowing people up and down a branch of the Hong Long Giang river, through one of the most gorgeous landscapes I was to see in Vietnam.

"I work seven days a week, from when the sun comes up in the morning to when the last job is done at night," she told me, astonished that a foreigner would be interested in the life of a peasant. "Most of our time is for working. There isn't much time for entertainment or talk. When I do talk to my friends, we talk about work and harvesting: whether the harvest is good or not; if there are shortages."

I wanted to know the most exciting thing that had happened in her lifetime. "My wedding day," she said with a toothy grin, almost blushing. But she refused to elaborate. "I've never been to Hanoi, but I've been to Ninh Binh [the nearest town]. Even though it's close, it's very difficult to get to."

Van confessed that, despite the toil, life was slowly improving for the people in her village. She ascribed this to the gradual abolition of the co-op system in favor of free-market farming since 1988. "In the old times, we worked together in the cooperative," she explained, guiding the boat around two young boys fishing in the river. "But now each family has its own rice fields. The size depends on how many people are in the family. Each family supervises its own work—like preparing seeds, plowing, planting, organizing insecticides—then harvesting the rice from the starting point to the end. In recent years, life has been getting a little better. They were hard times—when we worked in the big cooperative."

The payoff for the peasants was extra cash, which mostly went toward the purchase of newfangled consumer items. The most prized item was a television. "There are many in the village now," she said proudly. But one thing that irked Van was the price of livestock, which continued to outpace what farmers got for rice. Her family

Elders gather for an annual village festival on the outskirts of Hanoi.

In a country where almost everything is in short supply, nothing gets thrown away. Beer cans are recycled into a variety of household items, including toothbrush holders.

wanted to raise pigs, yet she considered the investment beyond their means.

"To buy a young pig costs a hundred thousand dong," she complained. "The pig can die. Then your investment is gone." She honestly considered her television a much better investment, inferring that it was somehow immortal. But her set was still new. She had yet to brave the twentieth-century frustration of a blown picture tube or some other electronic problem. Who was I to tell her that blind faith in technology doesn't last?

A strong wind whipped up dust devils along the highway into Vinh, leaving a shroud of orange dust on the surface of every leaf, sign, and vehicle. I quickly rolled up the window to keep from choking, but not before the thin organic mist had settled on my clothes and started to creep into my eyes, nose, and ears. With a sweep of the tongue across my lips, I could taste the bitterness of the land.

The journey from Thanh Hoa had been most revealing. Almost from the precise moment of our leaving the Red River valley, the landscape had taken on a deathly pallor, as if all life had been sucked away by some debilitating disease. The hillsides were devoid of trees, stripped bare not by bulldozers and chemical defoliants, as happened farther south, but by a flurry of logging in the rush to rebuild after the war, compounded by decades of overgrazing in league with slash-and-burn farming. Slender orange gullies scarred the hillsides, working their way ever deeper into the delicate top soil. Erosion was beginning to devour the landscape, as gangrene moves rapidly through an infected limb.

The prognosis wasn't much better for the flatlands of Nghe Tinh and Quang Binh provinces, the dozens of small alluvial plains that closely hug the coast. Here, the centuries-old rhythm of rice planting was still reeling from the effects of more than fifty years of continual war. Hundreds of bomb craters disfigure the paddy fields on either side of the highway and railroad line, some of them remnants of the French war but most the result of American air strikes against the vital supply and troop route to the south. Some of the bomb holes had been put to good use as fishponds or small reservoirs, but most of them lay untouched and unfilled, a lingering memorial to the hardship of years past and a persistent barrier to rural progress in years to come.

Young fishermen make their way across a bamboo bridge over the Yen River in Ha Son Binh province.

Residents in this region aren't especially unfriendly, but on the other hand they strain to exude a smile, almost as if the years of misery have fixed a mien of forlorn resignation on each face. They squat at the side of the road, peddling dust-covered fruit and vegetables; they toil through muddy fields behind water buffalo, straining to plow around the craters, praying they don't strike an unexploded bomb; they hack at the gaunt trees and shrubs with primitive axes, scraping together fuel for this evening's fire, but neglecting the fact that each bundle of firewood takes them a step farther down the road to environmental starvation.

As if history weren't enough to contend with, nature also conspires against the people of the central coast. Ask any Vietnamese, "Which part of your country has the foulest weather?" and the answer invariably will be the area around Vinh. Too far south to benefit from the protective shield of Hainan Island and too far north to gain advantage from the stormless belt on either side of the equator, the coast is pummeled by the unrepentant rage of typhoons each summer. Tidal waves rip away at the shore, submerging the coastal rice fields and leaving a thick crust of saline soil that must be leached before planting resumes. Farther inland, the resolute typhoons dump their excess water on the highlands, where there is little vegetation or soil left to absorb it. The water rushes down the hillsides, swelling rivers and streams, sweeping away bridges and whole villages, floods that further add to the plight of local farmers. When it isn't raining, there's drought. And once the tidal waves cease, the wind whips up a different sort of fury, dunes that can swell to twenty or thirty feet, a slow and silent assault on both crops and pastures.

The city offers meager salvation. Vinh was heavily bombed during both the French and American wars. Most of its vital structures were destroyed again and again, and thousands of its residents were killed, which gives some clue to the state of the urban landscape today. Vinh displays a perpetually unfinished demeanor, a place of temporary buildings that have yet to be replaced by more sturdy and permanent successors. Many of the homes are rebuilt in dreary white plaster or red brick, the cheapest and most abundant construction materials, and the municipal market and the theater resemble flimsy aircraft hangars—steel frames with thin metal shells that barely protect patrons from the elements. Dark figures hunker down at the edges of the hangars, people scrambling to make a living off the slim pickings of an exiguous land.

Yet in a wasteland there are often unseen riches, hidden beneath the soil or obscured in time. Such is the case with this central coast, which has at times thrown off the shackles of misery to produce articles of unforeseen beauty or brilliance. Despite the poverty and lack of natural resources, and disregarding the fact that everyday life has been uncompromising for many centuries, Vinh and its hinterland have given birth to some of the most important men in Vietnamese history.

Eighteenth-century poet Nguyen Du gave some indication of things to come. In such classic works of Vietnamese literature as *Kim Van Kieu* and *Calling the Wandering Souls*, he used a thin veil of romance and folktale to describe the agony of the peasants and the decadence of the corrupt mandarins who ruled over them, thereby setting up an archetype for grass-roots rebellion.

The mandarins were later superseded by French masters, but life in the central provinces didn't improve. Resentment against the French exploded into open rebellion in the final two decades of the nineteenth century, as Phan Dinh Phung and Phan Boi Chau staged bloody insurrections against the colonial overlords in Nghe An and Ha Tinh (later merged into a single province). The French had no problem quelling such minor disturbances, yet they sowed the seed for what would shortly follow.

Born into this smoldering furnace of revolution in 1890 was a boy named Nguyen Sinh Cung, son of a local mandarin who had been discharged from his government job after being accused of anti-French activities. The redundant civil servant volunteered to teach the village boys everything from mathematics to philosophy, with a hefty dose of anti-French rhetoric on the side. After his mother died in 1901, young Cung fell even more under the spell of his father. They moved four years later to Hue, the imperial capital, so that Cung could study at Quoc Hoc National Academy. It was there that he chose the first of his many aliases, Nguyen Tat Thanh.

Thanh left Vietnam in 1912 as a kitchen helper aboard a French steamer. His travels took him to New York and London and eventually to Paris, where he worked at various odd jobs and fell in with a clique of radical French intellectuals. As a bold and brash twenty-nine-year-old, Thanh talked his way into the Versailles Conference in 1919 and petitioned U.S. president Woodrow Wilson and other world leaders to liberate Vietnam from colonial rule. He even cited Wilson's own Fourteen Points declaration, which called for self-determination for all people. He was rebuffed, of course: in those days self-determination was for white men only. But it wasn't the last time that Thanh would turn to America for philosophical guidance or direct assistance.

Thanh soon changed his name to Nguyen Ai Quoc—"Nguyen the Patriot"—and in 1920, inspired by the Bolshevik Revolution in Russia, became one of the founding members of the French Communist Party. Having been rejected by the Americans, he ventured to Russia for further political training, then to China, which was in the midst of a gargantuan struggle between Nationalists and the nascent Communist movement. It was in the British crown colony of Hong Kong, on a fateful day in 1930, that Ai Quoc formed the Communist Party of Indochina with an avowed mission to destroy colonial rule and institute an egalitarian social and political system.

It wasn't long before the new doctrine took root in Ai Quoc's home province. The Great Depression was no small factor, forcing down market prices for commodities such as rubber and coal, on which the economy of French Indochina depended, and prompting plantation owners into even harsher treatment of their workers. Before the year was out, the peasants of Nghe Tinh revolted and successfully ousted their French landlords. Plantations in the province were transformed into rural cooperatives ("soviets"), all debts were canceled, and the Communists set up their own administration in Vinh. The French retaliated a year later, crushing the Nghe Tinh revolt and silencing its leaders via imprisonment or execution.

On the eve of World War II, Ai Quoc returned to Vietnam for the inaugural general meeting of the Indochina Communist Party, his first opportunity to meet and exchange ideas with other young revolutionaries from Nghe Tinh province. Now he changed his alias one last time, into a name that would inspire the masses. In English it translates into "He Who Enlightens," but in the original Vietnamese it reads Ho Chi Minh.

I spent an afternoon in Ho's birthplace, the Nam Dam district, about an hour's drive west of Vinh in the valley of the Song Ca River. In Ho's younger days this was a destitute district, but it has grown moderately well-off in modern times on the proceeds of tourism (the thousands who annually flock to see his birthplace) and government subsidies (to keep the historic buildings and their surroundings in top condition). Nam Dam is now a prosperous anomaly in a meager landscape, a lush area, much richer than the rest of Nghe Tinh province, with a multitude of livestock and emerald green rice paddies that sprawl in helter-skelter fashion to the horizon. The alluvial soil is dark and rich here, the fishing is good in the local ponds, and the people have time to stop and chat with visitors.

Ho Chi Minh was born in a tiny village called Chua, the nucleus of his mother's clan. The compound is looked after today by the local commune with the same reverence that Catholics would show toward a saintly shrine. Peanuts, apples, mulberries, and longans flourish in the garden, hemmed in by a fence of towering green bamboo. A buffalo munches on grass at the base of a betel nut palm. At the rear of the compound is a small house with a thatched roof and bamboo walls. Hardwood poles set on circular stones support the frame of the structure, and hardened clay serves perfectly well as the floor. "We feel fresh in these houses," explained my guide, a young woman with raven hair and a moon-shaped face who works for the local commune. Indeed, as we stood there talking, a gust of wind

Ho Chi Minh's ancestral home in the village of Chua near Vinh. This particular room belonged to his mother. The founder of modern Vietnam was born on a wooden bed in this house in 1890 and spent his first five years here. His name at birth was Nguyen Sinh Cung, but he later changed this to his famous alias Ho Chi Minh, which means "He Who Enlightens."

blew straight through, moderating the heat and humidity of midday.

Inside the house, one finds the bamboo bed on which Ho's mother gave birth to three children, the dowry chest where she kept her most precious possessions, and a loom for weaving silk cloth. "You see the oil lamp. That was used to produce light when Ho Chi Minh was a child. I don't think you have such lamps in America," smiled the woman. "We used to," I told her truthfully, although I don't think she believed me. "A long time ago. Back in the days when America was founded."

The utter modesty of the surroundings is manifest, so unpretentious as to make Mount Vernon and Monticello seem ostentatious in comparison. The father of the Vietnamese Revolution lived in a grass shack, slept on a bamboo bed. The fathers of the American Revolution—Washington and Jefferson—lived in state-of-the-art luxury of their day. Yet as disparate as their backgrounds were, they shared common goals and aspirations for their emerging nations. Given his colonial heritage and formative years in Paris, you would think that Ho Chi Minh would have used the French Revolution as his blueprint. Yet he rejected the French model as nothing more than a delusion, a senseless bloodbath that led to the tyranny of Napoleon rather than the liberation of the common people. Instead, we have the ultimate irony: Ho found his greatest inspiration in the American model of liberty.

"We hold these truths to be self-evident, that all men are created equal." This statement from the American Declaration of Independence was borrowed by Ho (with full credit) as one of the opening lines of his declaration of freedom from France, which he uttered before a half million people in Hanoi on September 2, 1945. His declaration is reprinted in Vietnamese newspapers on this day each year, and acknowledgment is still given to the founders of America for their inspiration to the Vietnamese cause.

It was in nearby Sen, the village of his father's clan, where Ho spent most of his preteenage life. Dark clouds had come up and a thunderstorm was brewing as I arrived. Teenagers from the commune scurried up and down ladders, lifting wooden shields into place to protect the delicate thatching on this second Ho Chi Minh homestead. I took refuge in the nearby museum, gazing at old black-and-white photos that depict the life story of the father of Vietnam. At the rear of the museum I found another structure, a shrine dedicated to the memory of Ho, a strange fusion of old-time religion and modern Communist dogma. At the center of the room was a huge bust of Ho, backed by a maroon curtain decorated with star and sickle. Previous visitors had left joss sticks burning inside brass pots at the base of the bust, or plates of oranges and lotus blossoms on the floor.

Over at the side of the room, on a low wooden table, I found the guest book. I flipped back through the year, curious to know who had preceded me to the birthplace of one of the great leaders of our time. An American priest, an Egyptian politician, two Cubans who evoked the struggles of José Marti and Fidel Castro in wishing Vietnam a "triumph on the road to socialism." A woman from Massachusetts wrote, "I'm very sorry for our part," while a retired lieutenant colonel in the U.S. Air Force said simply, "Thank you." But the most poignant message was left by an anonymous visitor: "You are here in the heart and mind of one American who was glad you were born."

TONKIN GULF INCIDENT

Although there had been U.S. "advisors" and support personnel in South Vietnam for several years, America wasn't drawn into a full-blown war until the infamous Tonkin Gulf Incident of 1964.

In early August of that year, the USS *Maddox* was on routine "eavesdropping" patrol in international waters in the Tonkin Gulf when it was confronted by torpedo boats of the North Vietnamese Navy. Shots were allegedly exchanged, but the American ship was unharmed. Two days later, the *Maddox* and another U.S. destroyer were attacked again in the same area.

President Lyndon Johnson ordered a retaliatory air strike against North Vietnamese positions and then went before the U.S. Congress to ask for emergency powers to use military force to "prevent further aggression" in Indochina. By a unanimous vote in the House of Representatives and an 88–2 majority in the Senate, the fateful Tonkin Gulf Resolution was passed, in effect a declaration of war on North Vietnam.

For the duration of the war, the U.S. Seventh Fleet stationed aircraft carrier battle groups at a position called Yankee Station at the lower end of the Gulf of Tonkin. The official name for this naval operation was Task Force 77. It normally included two to four flattops with a complement of about a hundred attack aircraft each. These carrier-based jets could easily undertake "aerial interdiction" of enemy supply lines and attack other strategic targets in the north. The planes most often called upon were the F-4 Phantom, A-4 Skyhawk, and A-6 Intruder. The fleet also helped coordinate and launch secret Navy SEAL commando missions along the North Vietnam coast.

Haiphong was the most important port on the Gulf of Tonkin, crucial to the North Vietnamese war effort as a vital link in the supply line from the Soviet Union and China. Carrier-based planes from the Seventh Fleet mined the harbor in 1972, effectively shutting down the port for eight months, until the Paris Peace Accord was signed in January 1973.

A SURPLUS OF EVIL

In the cobalt blue of predawn, we quit Vinh and headed east for the coast, to a place called Cua Lo, where we hoped to watch the fleet putting out to sea. Nguyen Van Thuan—a guide and translator who had accompanied me from Hanoi—roused a young man in a palm-leaf shack at the side of the road, and, sleepy-eyed, he pointed us farther up the beach, through a pine plantation and onto a sandy promontory that marked the outer limit of a murky bay. Sheltered within a hook-shaped estuary was the fleet, dark and brooding boats that bobbed up and down in the gentle swell. Yet there wasn't a fish-

OPPOSITE: As a morning storm brews on the South China Sea, fishing boats take shelter in the bay at Cua Lo north of Vinh.

Sunrise over the Gulf of Tonkin illuminates fishermen on the beach at Sam Son in Thanh Hoa province. The town doubles as a seaside resort popular with factory and school groups from Hanoi, who crowd the guest houses and cafes along the shore.

erman in sight. It was as if the boats were abandoned, a ghost fleet at anchor in a mystic harbor. There was utter silence except for the acute creaking of rope against wood and a rustle of wind through the nearby pines.

I shouted at the fishing boats in a rather random fashion until a head emerged from below one of the decks. When were they casting off? "Not today," barked the indignant fisherman. He turned his chin toward the Tonkin Gulf. "Can't you see there's a storm coming up. We're not going out today." Like a crab scuttling back into its den, his head disappeared in the darkness of the hold, and he slammed the hatch with a huff.

So we turned south, found the main highway again, and crossed the Song Lam estuary on a narrow pontoon bridge, into the panhandle of Nghe Tinh province. The desolation we had witnessed since before Vinh continued: the demolition of forests on every hillside, torrents of erosion, sand dunes clutching enviously at the rice fields, and the indiscriminate pattern of bomb craters through which the highway ran its undulating path. Adding to the feeling of oppression was an angry sky, blue-gray clouds that hovered low over the landscape, obscuring the peaks and higher mountain valleys. We navigated this diabolic gauntlet all the way down to the former DMZ.

The 17th parallel was like a homecoming for Thuan. Not that he held sentimental memories of what was once the Republic of South Vietnam, for Thuan was without doubt a tried-and-true son of Hanoi. Yet he had spent what he considered some of the best years of his life in this region. After being maimed in an American air strike along the Ho Chi Minh Trail, he had been seconded to the military press corps and attached to the Provisional Revolutionary Government (PRG) of South Vietnam, the political wing of the Viet Cong movement. From 1968 to 1975, this Communist regime in exile found refuge on the northern fringe of Quang Tri province, just inside the Demilitarized Zone.

Like many such boundaries, the 17th parallel is an arbitrary product of European gerrymandering. In this case, the Geneva Peace Conference of 1954 between France and Vietnam decided that this latitude (or more precisely, the Ben Hai River) would be a "temporary" dividing line between the Communist regime in the north and

The famous "17th Parallel Bridge" across the Ben Hai River once divided North and South Vietnam. A wide swath of land on either bank was designated the Demilitarized Zone (DMZ). Allegedly neutral, it was in reality the scene of deadly military activity throughout the Vietnam conflict. Highway One now rolls across the span on its long journey between Hanoi and Ho Chi Minh City.

the non-Communist government in the south. On either side of the line was a two-and-a-half mile buffer dubbed the Demilitarized Zone (DMZ) in which neither side was supposed to station troops. During the first few years of the American war, the DMZ was off limits to U.S. troops. Then in 1966 the North Vietnamese Army (NVA) moved five divisions into the zone and began to stage attacks against enemy positions in the south. For the remainder of the conflict, the DMZ was the site of heavy, often bloody, fighting.

We parked on the north shore of the Ben Hai River, and I walked across the span with Thuan. An old U.S. Army truck, converted to civilian use—but still olive green and with a faint white star visible on the driver's door—rumbled across the steel cantilever bridge on its way to the north. We stopped at midriver and gazed out over the former expanse of the DMZ. During the war this zone had seen almost daily action, particularly U.S. artillery and aircraft strikes against NVA positions and convoys. Yet now it was as tranquil as any rural landscape: emerald-green rice paddies, peasants fishing with bamboo poles, and children shouting in the background as they herded cows toward the river.

"It brings back many memories," said Thuan. "I came here often during the war. When we got word from Hanoi that a [foreign] delegation was coming, I rushed to come here. A lot of foreigners came, but just a few Americans. I remember when Jane Fonda and Tom Hayden came. I had to meet them and show them around."

Thuan pointed to a wooden house on the south bank and explained that during the war it had served as a reception center for visitors to the PRG zone. "After 1968, the Americans never came up this far. They drew a definite line at the next river down [the Cam Lo]." He sniffed at the wind and pointed southward. "Down on that ridge was the American artillery base at Gio Linh and over there, to the west, that was the famous U.S. Marine base called Con Tien."

Without warning, Thuan broke into a low, mournful tune. I thought it was a dirge for fallen comrades, but he quickly corrected me. "It's a love song," he smiled. "Between the people living on either side of the Ben Hai River. It was written during the war. They used to play it on the radio a lot, and we all knew the words. It's from one brother to another, from a husband to his wife, from a father to his son—people and families who were divided by the DMZ."

The little herder kids had gathered around us by now, listening to Thuan's heartfelt song. He asked them to join in, but they merely shrugged indifference. "The children don't even know this song," he lamented, still lost in his memories of the war. "They know nothing of the past. This is the new generation."

I'm not one to put much faith in the tangibility of ghosts and spirits. But after several days in Quang Tri province, I started to believe that there was something perfectly evil about the place. It wasn't any single incident, more an overall suspicion that grew stronger with each day. I would part the curtains of my hotel window in Dong Ha, peer out at the former DMZ, and think: There's something out there, something inhuman and invisible and thoroughly wicked, the ghosts of war hovering close to the ground.

In most of Vietnam you can easily escape the memories of war. The crops are thriving, the hamlets have been rebuilt, the postwar generation gets on with the business of making a living. But in Quang Tri province the past cannot be ignored, no matter how large the blinders. Vast tracts of the province look as they did when the Americans left in 1973. It's safe to say that with the possible exceptions of Beirut and Baghdad, no place on earth has so much lingering war damage. Defoliation is pervasive, conspicuous damage on every hillside caused by bulldozers, napalm, Agent Orange and other toxic chemicals. Where tropical forest used to thrive, only elephant grass and weeds now grow. The mountaintops are unnaturally level, sheared off to make way for U.S. fire bases or landing zones. In Gio Linh, at the side of the highway, the rusting, burned-out hulk of an American battle tank is being used as one wall of a farmhouse. At a pepper cooperative on the site of Camp Carroll, onetime headquarters of U.S. forces along the DMZ, peasant workers use howitzer shell casings as metal siding for their shacks. All along Highway Nine, the route from the coast to the Laotian border beyond Khe Sanh, there are heaps of memories—rusted shell casings, grenade fragments, ammunition boxes, and vehicle parts—a harvest of metal for scrap dealers. Thuan caught me staring out at the bleakness of the DMZ. He tapped me on the shoulder and said, "We call this the land where dogs eat stones and the chickens eat gravel. Nothing will grow here."

Equally disturbing is Quang Tri town , a thriving provincial capital in former times but now little more than an urban skeleton. The old walled city—once a tightly packed warren of imperial Vietnamese and French colonial buildings—is now a wasteland of

Military scrap heaps line Highway Nine between Dong Ha and Khe Sanh. The debris includes everything from rusty bomb fragments and ammunition boxes to live grenades and mines. Peasants collect the metal from the surrounding jungle and farmland, hoping to sell it to scrap dealers from the city. But it's a dangerous occupation: hundreds of people have been killed or maimed by exploding ordnance.

weeds and crumbling buildings, infested by snakes and live ordnance. Nearby, the Roman Catholic cathedral lies in ruins, its bell tower blown to bits. A cement crucifix in the driveway is riddled with bullet holes and blast marks, barely able to stand. Throughout the town you find the same utter destruction.

"You want to know what happened in Quang Tri? I'll tell you," said a young man I met in the "temporary" town market—temporary now for nearly twenty years. "I remember when there were eighty-two days and nights of fighting and destruction. The amount of bombs dropped on Quang Tri in 1972 was equivalent to seven Hiroshimas. And I remember before that, when this was a beautiful city with an active market, with boats coming and going along the river. Quang Tri had fifty thousand people in the old days. It was so busy. But now there are maybe twelve thousand. That's all. The rest are dead or gone."

Quang Tri was a victim of the so-called "Eastertide" offensive of March 1972, when two Communist divisions poured south from the DMZ. They overwhelmed the South Vietnamese Army (ARVN) defenders, capturing the city without much of a fight. A month later, Saigon troops counterattacked, but it took them five months—and hundreds of U.S. air strikes—to recapture the town. It was a classic example of the American war axiom: "We had to destroy the town in order to save it."

Later in the day I met the mayor of Quang Tri, a kind man with gray hair, soft eyes, and a gentle smile. His wasn't an easy job. He explained that after the war Quang Tri had been combined into a single province with Hue. Most of the government aid for reconstruction had been siphoned off by provincial authorities for the old imperial city. He bore no grudges: Hue was the cultural heart of Vietnam and should take priority. But there was never enough money left over for Quang Tri. Still, the city was progressing bit by bit. The mayor was most proud that a new covered market would open in a few months.

I asked if the town would throw a party in honor of the new market. "No, we won't," the mayor responded in a sorrowful voice. "We can't afford that, even a small celebration. We must use all our resources to rebuild the town." Then he proffered a line that I heard again and again on my travels through Vietnam. "We want to have reconciliation with the people of America so that they can help us rebuild." This wasn't some insipid concept mouthed by a government official; it was a genuine plea, straight from the heart. A comment on perhaps the greatest irony of modern warfare: that the worst of enemies can become the best of friends. A concept on which many Vietnamese seem to stake the entire future of their country.

We took an extra day and drove up to Khe Sanh, tracing the undulating path of Highway Nine on its route through the foothills. This was to be my farthest penetration into the Central Highlands, the closest I would get to Laos. History alone compelled me: I wanted to see one of the most famous battlegrounds of American history, a place steeped in Marine Corps legend, the foreign field that Bruce Springsteen sings about in "Born in the U.S.A.," his anthem to the Vietnam vet.

The route is littered with minor battlefields and former bases, places that now boast little more than memories. Wind lashed at my face as I walked across the sheared-off crest of Hill 241, named, like most American landing zones and fire bases, after its height (in meters) above sea level. Hill 241 was not chemically defoliated, rather it was burned and bulldozed, and then sown with waist-high elephant grass. Such wonderful stuff, elephant grass: it could be burned off quickly to provide a clear field of fire and had the extra benefit of thwarting the regeneration of native plants. Two decades after cessation of hostilities, elephant grass still dominates the landscape. Only recently have workers from the local cooperative begun to slash the grass, planting lemon and eucalyptus trees that thrive in the rust-colored laterite soil. Roaming across the summit of Hill 241, I found an ammo box, shreds of sandbags and camouflage clothing, and a few howitzer casings, but little else to remind me that GIs had been here not so long ago.

Farther along, we stopped briefly for tea at a roadside stall in the Dung Long Valley. The proprietor was a young man by the name of Ho Van Hoa, a member of the Bru Van Kieu minority tribe. Asking in jest if he was named after the father of Vietnam, I was somewhat astonished to learn that indeed he was. All of the Bru Van Kieu people were named after Ho, having adopted this as their collective surname during the American war.

"My grandfather and father lived in this valley, and now myself," Hoa explained. "During the war, I was in Hue. But we came

Tobacco is one of the most important crops of Lang Cat village, but the Bru Van Kieu only grow it for their own use in self-rolled cigarettes and bamboo pipes.

back in 1975, after the liberation. I've been a farmer all these years. It's still very tough living here. When we get extra money, we buy rice. Farming here is very poor because of war destruction, insects, and wild animals. Like wild pigs. They dig up our cassava plants. We have locusts, too. And there are still minefields. It's very dangerous trying to be a farmer in this place."

Which is why Hoa and his wife had decided to develop a roadside café. "We've been open just three months. We sell cigarettes and drinks, and prepare meals. I have a meal ready now; do you want to eat?" I politely declined, and he continued. "We make about five thousand dong (eighty cents) a day. After three months, I'm not sure if this [the cafe] is a good idea or not. But so far we have increased our income." Another sideline was scrap, a natural outgrowth of life in Quang Tri province. Hoa buys from peasants who collect bits of metal from the former battlefields and American bases. He gets roughly forty dong (half a cent) a pound from itinerant scrap merchants who make the rounds of this and other valleys in the region.

Just then another farmer joined us in the simple wooden shack. His right arm was severed below the elbow. "This happened in 1980," he announced, almost a boast, as if his missing limb were the result of a war injury. "I was plowing a field and discovered a mine. I tried to defuse it, but it exploded. It happens all the time around here," he said matter-of-factly. "Mostly it's buffalo that get killed."

At Da Krong junction, we crossed a blue suspension bridge over a river of the same name. The road on the far side disappeared into a lush tropical valley, where towering trees of a dozen shades of green cling precipitously to the edge of sheer mountains. This was the rain forest of my imagination, as it exists elsewhere in Southeast Asia, untouched by defoliant, unscarred by napalm. The road was different too: relatively new and devoid of potholes, a rare phenomenon in today's Vietnam.

"This is a new highway, built with Cuban help," said Thuan, and once again he lapsed into a nostalgic haze. "It follows one of the sections of the Ho Chi Minh Trail. The Americans never had any permanent base in this valley. That's why there's so much jungle. They just sent in helicopters or platoons on foot. This valley was always under *our* control."

People who weren't here during the war usually have rather

Mung beans dry in the sun at Lang Cat, a tiny village below the Khe Sanh Plateau populated by about 300 members of the Bru Van Kieu minority group. The villagers also cultivate rice, millet, cassava, bananas, and ground nuts, in addition to raising water buffalo, chickens, pigs, and cattle.

distorted notions of the Ho Chi Minh Trail. They hear that trucks and jeeps and other vehicles used this route and picture it as some sort of primitive superhighway. They consider the term "trail" and assume it was a single path. In actuality, the Ho Chi Minh Trail was a network of five long parallel roads with twenty-one axes, totaling more than 12,500 miles. Vehicles could proceed only with the utmost difficulty; much of the cargo was carried on the backs of men rather than in trucks.

Although it wasn't known by the Americans until after the war, the trail was active as early as 1959 as a Communist infiltration route to the south. More than thirty thousand soldiers and youth volunteers worked on its construction, hacking a path from virgin jungle while battling heat, malaria, and malnutrition. The trail began just over the DMZ, in the southwest corner of Dong Hoi province, where the road and railway line from Hanoi came to an end. Using the Truong San mountains as a shield, the trail ran south, mostly across the border in Laos and Cambodia, but with significant spurs inside South Vietnam. A six-hundred-mile stretch of the trail in Laos was the main conduit, more than twenty-six feet wide and able to take big supply trucks and armored vehicles. Another little-known fact is the existence of a three-thousand-mile-long pipeline that ran alongside the trail to supply fuel along the route. Without a doubt, it is one of the great engineering efforts of the twentieth century.

The Americans tried to bomb the trail into oblivion during successive operations. The most famous of these attempts was Rolling Thunder, from 1965 to 1968, during which time more than 643,000 tons of bombs rained down upon the route and its environs. The linchpin of Rolling Thunder was the B-52 bomber; the code name of the operation derives from the din of B-52s carpet bombing a destructive path across the land.

Thuan was a victim of one of those strikes. He had been a soldier in the North Vietnamese Army, assigned to a mobile antiaircraft crew sent down the Ho Chi Minh Trail to support troop and supply movements. But his active service was short-lived. As we drove along this newly paved stretch of the trail, he told his story. "I was one of four people that operated a 12mm antiaircraft gun. I injured my arm in a B-52 attack. It was almost severed. The doctors sewed it back on, but I lost twenty kilos [forty-four pounds] and lots of blood, too. I remember, I went down to Kontum province in the back of a

truck. But after my injury, I walked three months to get back to the north. We ate rice along the way, which we mixed with whatever we could find in the jungle—wild bananas, roots, and things such as that."

Khe Sanh itself was a bit of a disappointment. I don't know what I expected to find, a monument or a museum or something to mark history. There were no bunkers or barracks or other military buildings, merely the ubiquitous heaps of rusting military scrap. The old Marine Corps airfield was still there, taken over by the Vietnamese Army and off-limits to civilians. "The Marines ripped out the tarmac and took it away when they left," said Thuan with a sly smile. "But we brought it back from Dong Ha after liberation and made the field new again."

We drove out as far as Lang Vei, site of the famous U.S. Special Forces base, from where we had a splendid view of the majestic purple mountains of Laos. The only token of war is defoliation, the barren hills that ring the valley. Yet on this particular day, with the sun out and billowy clouds set against a blue silken sky, Khe Sanh seemed to take on the glaze of summer in the Scottish Highlands rather than the weary war-torn feel of central Vietnam.

Khe Sanh is prospering in its own modest way, as a staging point on what is becoming a very important international trade route. Huge trucks lumber through the valley, laden with tropical hardwoods from the forests of Laos. The truckers are tired and hungry. Their machines need fuel. The people of Khe Sanh provide for their needs with a profusion of new shops, cafés, and service stations, and the peasants sell bunches of bananas and jackfruit at the side of the road. There isn't the downtrodden atmosphere one finds elsewhere in Quang Tri. In fact, you could drive through this valley without gleaning the slightest hint of the carnage that took place here during three notorious months of 1968. The ghosts of war have been purged from Khe Sanh.

SIEGE OF KHE SANH

There are striking similarities between the historic siege at Dien Bien Phu in 1954 and that of Khe Sanh in 1968. Both were in isolated mountain valleys of no critical importance until they became strategically entwined in the operation of vital Communist supply routes. In both cases, Western armies miscalculated native troop strength and their own ability to wage war in jungle-covered mountains. And in each instance the foreign forces were completely surrounded and cut off from reinforcements. Unlike the French who surrendered at Dien Bien Phu, the Americans won the seige of Khe Sanh— although in the end it was a Pyrrhic victory.

Khe Sanh was one of a series of American fire bases along the DMZ, situated in a broad mountain valley near the Laos border and sitting between two branches of the Ho Chi Minh Trail. Its strategic importance to both sides was manifest. From the time the first U.S. troops set foot in the valley in 1962, there was sporadic fighting. But things didn't heat up until 1967 when General William Westmoreland, commander-in-chief of U.S. forces in Vietnam, began pondering an invasion of southern Laos to sever the Ho Chi Minh Trail. While the general waited for President Johnson and Congress to approve his controversial scheme, Westmoreland ordered a massive infusion of U.S. Marines and South Vietnamese Rangers. Troop strength had reached six thousand by Christmas.

What the Americans did not know was that the North Vietnamese Army (NVA) was secretly massing four divisions and some twenty thousand troops in the Khe Sanh area in anticipation of the upcoming Tet Offensive. Some military historians now believe that the Communist buildup at Khe Sanh was staged to distract American forces from the real objectives of the Tet Offensive: the capture of South Vietnamese cities.

The NVA launched their assault in January, using entrenched artillery in coordination with massive ground attacks, as they had fourteen years earlier at Dien Bien Phu. Their new secret weapon was the Russian-made T-76 tank, which they used to crush the U.S. Army Special Forces camp at Lang Vei in early February. But the Marines countered with a staunch defense that for seventy-seven days rebuffed repeated attacks. On April 7 the U.S. Army First Air Cavalry Division came to the relief of the beleaguered leathernecks. A week later, the siege ended. The Marines counted 205 dead; no accurate tally of NVA dead was ever achieved, although estimates range as high as 15,000.

The irony is that Westmoreland never got permission for his incursion into Laos. The fire base at Khe Sanh was abandoned three months later. The Americans blew up their bunkers and ripped up the runway. They never returned.

It was our last morning in Quang Tri province. Thuan and the driver sat down at the breakfast table with broad grins, eager to tell me how they had both had the same dream last night. Not a nightmare, but a good dream. With a solemn face and a deadpan voice, Thuan revealed how a vision of heavenly bliss had come to them in their sleep: a female fairy with a perfect figure shrouded in a silk *ao dai*, an oval face with porcelain skin, long eyelashes, and raven hair that flowed down around her shoulders.

It's not difficult to comprehend why a man would wish to dream about a beautiful woman. But Thuan discarded the face value of his vision and launched into an ardent explanation of its much deeper meaning. In Vietnam, it seems, there are two types of fairies who come in the night. A hideous male fairy with a long beard and a walking stick is a very bad portent indeed. But a ravishing female fairy is a harbinger of good fate; she gives you strength and courage to proceed in your endeavor. "We needed the determination to complete our long journey to Ho Chi Minh City," Thuan said with absolute earnestness. "Now we have it."

Such an atavistic attitude seemed odd coming from the mouth of an avowed Communist, someone who wasn't supposed to believe in God, not to mention good and bad fairies. Thuan never let on whether he took much stock in folktales, but such stories give some indication of how traditional Vietnamese beliefs—based on ancient concepts gleaned from nature, Buddhism, and Taoism—simmer just below the surface of the Marxist-Leninist state. There are diehard Communists in Vietnam, make no mistake about that, but the mass of the common people, and many a cadre, are indelibly tied to a much

A young bride.

OPPOSITE: Despite extensive work undertaken by the Vietnamese government and UNESCO since the end of the Vietnam War, much of the Citadel remains in ruins. Much of this ancient gateway behind Hung Mieu Temple has been reclaimed by the jungle.

older legacy. For them, Communism is not so much an everyday reality (especially now that the rural co-op system is breaking down) but an alien cult practiced by the bureaucratic high priests of Hanoi, its own sort of fairy story.

Thuan was a flawless example of the duality I found throughout Vietnam. He was explicitly proud of his service during the war and his membership in the Communist Party; but equally, he reveled in his peasant stock, the fact that his mother and father were farmers, that he had grown up on the land, and that he knew a thing or two about ancient ways. Thuan went out of his way to demonstrate that he wasn't a city boy. His whole train of thought seemed to stem from the soil and the woods. He was constantly pointing out this crop or that, explaining when it was planted, how it was harvested, the various ways in which it was used. Around every bend in the highway, we seemed to come across something that inspired a new folktale, no doubt drawn from his youth in the country.

We left Dong Ha after breakfast and turned south in the direction of Hue, following a stretch of highway that the dispirited French had dubbed the "Street Without Joy" because of the fierce Viet Minh resistance in the area. But this was also "The Way of the Mandarins," the route by which nobles and artists had made their way to the imperial court in Hue, a fact that reminded Thuan of yet another fairy story: "A husband left his wife in the village and went to Hue to study to become a mandarin. But he was a failure and became a wandering beggar instead. One night, a fairy came and visited the wife in her dreams. This gave her hope and determination to search for her long-lost husband. She took to the road and eventually found him, and they returned to live the rest of their lives in their village." The moral of this story seemed a bit nebulous to me, but, as usual, Thuan was quick to explain. "Not everyone who goes to Hue becomes a mandarin," he smiled. He thought that was an important lesson for me to keep in mind.

Hue is like a hologram: the image depends on your angle of view. Hold it in one light, inspect it, what do you see? A city of gardens, an urban canvas replete with lotus ponds, dark tree-shaded avenues, and the tantalizing smell of spring blossoms, where reverence for nature reaches a peculiar apex after death, as friends of the deceased garland his favorite shrubs and trees with silk ribbons. A

An evening storm drenches commuters heading home across the Trang Tien Bridge in central Hue.

city of the arts, which gave birth to a unique Vietnamese mode of decoration, a style imbued with images of mythical creatures, ostentatious adornments, and Kodachrome colors, a sort of oriental baroque. A river city, spread along the banks of the slow-flowing Perfume River, which is filled to the brim with small wooden boats—used for fishing and cargo and ferrying humans—and crossed by two mighty spans that have a history all their own. A city for scholars, too, with a dozen institutes of higher learning and the country's preeminent high school, where many of Vietnam's leaders of the last two centuries were educated and molded into future heads of state And in some respects a city of sorrow, a flagrant reminder of the Vietnam that could have been, a national identity that is still struggling to emerge.

Human figure class at the Hue Art College. Hue has long been the fulcrum of education in Vietnam, with a dozen institutes of higher education that cater to a wide variety of interests. Students dominate the parks and cafes along the south bank of the Perfume River and play football on the grounds of the old Citadel.

This is a city that lies at the very core of the Vietnamese consciousness, a place that radiates culture in all its many-splendored forms to the far-flung corners of the land. Scholars long to study in Hue; young monks yearn to enter a monastery here. Newlyweds are drawn by the romantic essence, while tourists flock here to behold the intrinsic brilliance of Vietnamese civilization.

Hue is also an incomparable—and somewhat involuntary—unifier of north and south, perhaps the only place in Vietnam that can claim that distinction. Residents of Hanoi and the Red River valley have a traditional disdain for their counterparts in Saigon and the Mekong Delta, appraising them as crude cousins who have been irretrievably corrupted by the false promises of materialism. Southerners, on the other hand, see their opposite numbers in the north as definitive bores, their minds set in the cement of Communist orthodoxy, their hearts frozen by fifty years of economic and cultural chill. Yet people from either end of the geographical and political spectrum agree that Hue is something special. Wherever I went in Vietnam people would ask, "Have you been to Hue? Have you seen it? Isn't it wonderful?"—not giving me a chance to respond. They would launch into marvelous descriptions of Hue and its manifold monuments, only to confess (when asked) that they had never actually been there. No place else in Vietnam has such a mythological hold.

For hundreds of years various factions struggled to claim Hue as their own. A pawn in Vietnam's turbulent history that was fought over by rival dynasties from north and south, the city can be traced to its roots in the early fourteenth century, when the region below the Perfume River was annexed by armies of the powerful Tran dynasty. They founded a settlement called Phu Xuan (later changed to Hue) that served as a frontier outpost to the lands of Champa. Then in 1636, after the gradual disintegration of Vietnam into separate spheres, Hue became capital of the southern Nguyen dynasty. This was the dawn of the city's first great golden age, when "luxury prevailed," according to court historian Le Quy Don. "Houses were sculptured, walls built of stone, hangings and curtains made of silk, plates and dishes of bronze or porcelain, furniture of precious wood, harnesses were ornamented with gold and silver."

Yet prosperity was short-lived, as the dynasty crumbled beneath its own decadence and the south collapsed into a thirty-year peasant revolt called the Tay Son Epoch. What eventually emerged from this period of chaos was not a popular regime of farmers and fishermen but the second Nguyen dynasty. In 1802, newly crowned emperor Gia Long, the first of the Nguyen kings, made Hue his imperial capital and ordered the construction of a huge new citadel and palace complex. This was the onset of an uninterrupted century-and-a-half of splendor when Hue was the locus of cultural, religious, and regal power in Vietnam.

There was a time, not all that long ago, when imperial edict determined nearly everything that transpired in Hue. The emperor was secluded behind the three concentric walls of the Citadel, segregated from mere mortals within his Purple Palace and pampered like some living god by an army of prostrating servants. The emperor lived

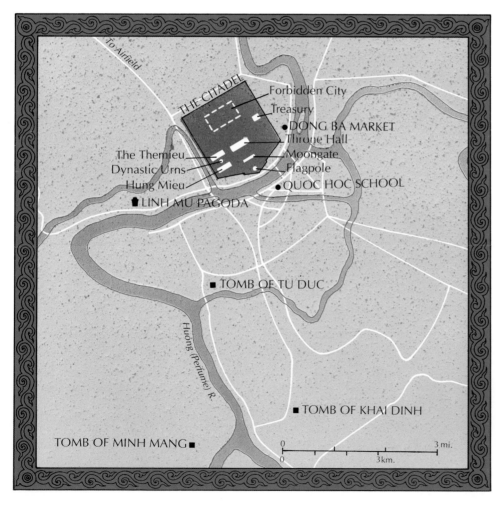

Hue and vicinity.

in what was called the "heaven" area, while the queen resided in the "earth" zone. Only members of the royal family and a select group of royal servants were allowed to pass this far into the Forbidden City. There were over a hundred buildings in total, arranged along a central axis, with military headquarters on the west and civilian offices for education, culture, and government on the east.

The Nguyen kings were notoriously opulent, aping the style of the even more flamboyant Manchu rulers of China. They lived in unabashed luxury, surrounding themselves with beautiful treasures, adorning their bodies in the most sumptuous clothes. As Le Quy Don noted, "They regarded gold and silver as sand, rice as dirt." Many priceless dynastic items are preserved in the Museum of Antique Objects inside the Citadel in Hue: royal seals in the shape of dragons, ivory whiskey decanters, a silver betel-nut case, and a miniature golden tree made with glass leaves; the golden palanquin of Bao Dai; a teakwood bureau at which Tu Duc once worked, and the imperial garments of Khai Dinh—a yellow silk robe covered in solid gold embroidery and fastened with gold buttons.

Yet not content just to immerse themselves in material things, the emperors also collected human treasures. Invited to live at the court were all the best poets and painters in the land, who at once became privileged mandarins with a royal stipend that allowed them to cultivate their arts. It was by this means that Hue became the cultural heart of Vietnam. And also its garden: the artists and intellectuals were directed to bring plants from their native regions to be replanted along the royal roads of Hue as a symbol of national unity. The mandarins also brought recipes from every region, which transformed Hue into the culinary capital, too.

Very rarely did the emperor expose himself to public scrutiny. Every three years, during the Festival of the Sacrifice of Heaven (a ceremony of the Cult of the Sky and the Earth), he would make his way by means of an undulating procession to an open-air altar called the Nam Giao, beyond the south bank of the Perfume River, where he would make humble submission to the gods. Every so often, the royal personage would proceed to a brick arena to watch gruesome combat between tigers and elephants—considered the "sport of kings" by the Nguyens. The last ghastly spectacle of this "sport" was held as late as 1904, by which time there weren't enough tigers left in the nearby jungles to provide a steady supply of contestants.

Detail from one of the nine bronze urns that sit in front of the Hung Mieu Temple in the Citadel. Cast in the 1830s, the urns depict the history of early Nguyen dynasty emperors like Gia Long, who founded the imperial city at Hue.

But the most auspicious royal occasion was Tet, the lunar new year, when the emperor was obliged to conduct a ceremony in the stone courtyard in front of the Forbidden City. Somerset Maugham witnessed the unfolding of this liturgy in the late 1920s, during the waning years of Nguyen power. "In the large open space soldiers in bright and fantastic uniforms were lined up, and in front of them two lines of mandarins according to their rank, the civil on the right and the military on the left," Maugham relates in "The Gentleman in the Parlour." "A little below were the eunuchs and the imperial orchestras; and on each side was a royal elephant in state caparison with a man holding a state umbrella over the howdah. The mandarins were dressed in Manchu fashion in high boots with thick white soles, silk robes splendidly embroidered, with voluminous sleeves, and black hats decorated with gold. Bugles blew, and we, the Europeans, crowded into the throne room. . . . The Emperor sat on a dais. In his gold robes he sank into the gold of the throne and the gold back cloth of the canopy over it so that at first you were hardly conscious that a living person was there."

This decadence was rudely terminated in 1945, when Bao Dai abdicated in favor of the Democratic Republic of Vietnam under the

Dragons descend a staircase at the back of the Purple Palace ruins. At the top of the stairs is a shrine dedicated to the water ghost and the old North Gate of the Citadel.

The outer wall and a brass cauldron are among the few remains of the Purple Palace, the inner sanctum of imperial power for more than a hundred years. Modeled after the Forbidden City in Beijing, where only members of the royal family and their personal servants were allowed inside, the palace was bombed by the French during the 1950s and then completely destroyed in the Tet Offensive of 1968.

For over a hundred years, no mere mortal could set foot inside the walls of the Purple Palace, the innermost sanctum of the imperial Citadel. Today, peasants till cassava and other crops in the bomb-shattered remains of the royal palace.

leadership of Ho Chi Minh. Although the French tried to restore him to the throne in 1950, Bao Dai was forced into exile four years later on the eve of the final French defeat. The royal Citadel was severely damaged during the French war, then nearly wiped away during the Tet Offensive of 1968 and the subsequent American counterattack. In little more than two decades, most of the physical and spiritual manifestations of imperial Vietnam were extinguished

Today the Nguyen kings are denounced for "reactionary feudalist policies" that humiliated and impoverished the peasantry and brought Vietnam into the disrepute of foreign domination. Nevertheless, even ardent Communists see Hue for what it is: a cultural and artistic gem that should be preserved for future generations, both as a caution to the abuse of power and a monument to the creative genius of Vietnam. Being well aware of its gross intemperance, today's citizens are not so much proud of their imperial past as they are fascinated by its utter eccentricity—in much the same way that the modern French may revel in the legacy of Napoleon.

The government is urgently trying to restore the Citadel and other parts of Hue to their former splendor. Not for occupation by the seventy-nine-year-old Bao Dai, the last emperor—who still lives in exile in France—but as a huge open-air museum for the enjoyment and education of both Vietnamese and foreign visitors. Reconstruction is an arduous task, as historians or archaeologists working on the project are quick to point out. Their endowment is enormous: over three hundred separate historic structures covering a combined area of 5.3 million acres.

"Our government considers Hue as the biggest conservation site in Vietnam," Chai Cong Nguyen told me as we sipped beers on the terrace of a café along the banks of the Perfume River. "That is why the state has invested money in restoring Hue. We have made a technical and economic plan that has been presented to the government. We are asking what can be done. But frankly, we have problems in finance."

Chai, a soft-spoken man with a bookish intellect, is director of the Hue Cultural and Historic Monument Preservation Office, the body responsible for garnering restoration funds and putting the money to best use. Hanoi has already provided 500 million dong ($100,000) for the renewal of ten historic buildings and the maintenance of fifty-one others. Another 600 million dong ($120,000) is slated for the refurbishment of eight additional structures during the 1990s, including the famous Noon Gate (Ngo Mon) at the front of the Citadel, the Shrine of the Nguyen Dynasty (Mieu Temple), and the Imperial Library (Thai Binh Lau).

Yet the cash-strapped Vietnamese realize they cannot fund the massive project on their own. They have turned overseas for assistance. UNESCO has set up a working group to oversee the restoration efforts and recently provided a specialist to survey the remains of the Purple Palace, in addition to donating vehicles, office equipment, and metal roofing to protect fragile historic sites. But that falls far short of the $4 million the Vietnamese hope to glean from international donors.

One of the most important concerns is that the renovation be true to history, using the same designs and fabrics as in the original structures. To achieve this, Chai has created a workshop within the Citadel to produce tiles, bricks, and other building materials by ancient means. "We are trying to make the materials the same way as they did in the old days—even though there are a hundred different kinds of tiles and bricks found at these sites," said Chai, who studied literature at Hue University before becoming a restoration expert fifteen years ago. "We go for the same shape, color, and texture—the highest principle of restoration. As you know, it's exhausting. But we are trying our best, and in years to come we will try to find even better ways to restore the ancient city."

Chai and his colleagues admit they still don't have the funds to carry out their most ambitious scheme: a ten-year plan to restore the entire Citadel, including the Grandmother's Palace (Truong Sanh), the Palace of Everlasting Longevity (Dien Tho), and the devastated Purple Palace, now a cassava field encompassed by crumbling walls. "Just for Bien Can Chanh—the first hall of the Purple Palace—restoration is estimated to cost $1.3 million," Chai remarked, with no small lament in his voice.

How do you rebuild a structure like the Purple Palace that has virtually vanished? This is where French authorities are lending a hand. Slumbering in various Parisian archives are detailed blueprints and photographs of the royal sites before their destruction. For instance, the original plans for the Bien Can Chanh are now in the Oriental Museum in Paris, where they have been housed since 1925 when the structure won first prize in an international design competition. Experts from Japan and Holland are helping to catalog and restore smaller historic items—statues, furniture, cannon, cauldrons, and other objects—found on site but now sheltered in warehouses or the Museum of Antique Objects.

Also badly in need of restoration are the seven imperial tombs, arrayed along the Perfume River on the outskirts of Hue. In many respects, because they were little touched by war, the tombs are more indicative of the grandeur of the royal Vietnamese court than the Citadel. Opinions vary on which is the most splendid, but three are a cut above the others: those of emperor Minh Mang (who ruled 1820–41), Tu Duc (1847–83), and Khai Dinh (1916–25).

The royal necropolis was far more than just a burial place. The area around each tomb was laid out with lavish gardens, temples, and pavilions that the emperor could enjoy during his lifetime. You might say these grounds functioned as quiet country retreats away from the propriety and protocol of the Citadel. Today, they are among the most pleasant gardens to be found anywhere in Vietnam. The immaculate gardens around Minh Mang's tomb are laid out in the shape of the Chinese character for eternity, although the catacomb is still sealed and overgrown with tropical vegetation. Tu Duc's

The Tomb of Tu Duc is one of the more impressive features of the royal necropolis on the banks of the Perfume River south of Hue. The massive stone slab in this photo is a biography of Tu Duc, who ruled Vietnam from 1848 to 1883 at the very pinnacle of Nguyen dynasty power in Indochina. More than 3,000 workers and craftsmen labored for three years to build the tomb, a miniature royal palace, waterfront pavilions, and lush gardens that the emperor used as a private pleasure ground until his death.

grave is set on the shores of a lotus pond with a small wooden pavilion where the emperor composed poetry and watched the performances of dance and musical troupes. A complete contrast in mood and style is the tomb of Khai Dinh. The architecture flaunts peculiar touches of European influence rather than the heavy dose of Chinese design that predominates elsewhere in the necropolis. Khai Dinh's burial chamber is a stunning tribute to royal opulence, with a golden effigy of the ruler surmounting a marble dais in the center of the room.

Like most everyone else in Vietnam, the guardians of old Hue are hoping for future American aid. "One of the things we hope for is that normal relations between Vietnam and the United States will come soon," said Chai as we shook hands. "As you see, culture is the bridge to connect nations and to repair old wounds."

Perhaps the imperial days have passed, but their memory lives on in the home of two of the last royal servants, Pham Van Thiet and his wife Pham Thi Nguyen, who reside in a two-story villa on the south side of Hue. Now in their seventies, they first met within the confines of the palace more than half a century ago on the eve of the Second World War. Thiet was valet to the emperor Bao Dai; Nguyen was a

Khai Dinh was the last Nguyen emperor to die in Vietnam (1925), and his ostentatious tomb crowns a hill above the Perfume River. But he was no more than a figurehead—a puppet of the French colonial authorities who held the real reins of power in Indochina—and the heavy rococo-style ornamentation of his tomb reflects his desire to blend French and Vietnamese culture.

Visiting students and workers from Ho Chi Minh City picnic inside the stelae house at Khai Dinh's Tomb. The stone slab tells the story of Khai Dinh's brief reign (1916–1925). He was succeeded by his son, Bao Dai, who abdicated in 1954 and now lives in exile in France.

A portrait of Khai Dinh in royal regalia sits behind a huge bronze urn in the Phong Tho Vua, or King's Chamber, of the emperor's tomb.

Madame Pham Thi Nguyen kneels before a shrine dedicated to her former employer Doan Huy, mother of Bao Dai, the last emperor of Vietnam. Nguyen and her husband look after a villa where the queen mother lived from the dissolution of the monarchy in 1954 until her death in 1980. But their relationship with the royal family goes back to the 1930s, when they both worked as servants in the Purple Palace.

royal cook. "I went to stay with the imperial family in the Citadel when I was fifteen years old," recalls Thiet. "I was allowed into the Purple Palace. I helped the emperor with anything he needed—cleaning and cooking; serving tea, coffee and his pipe; bringing playing cards. There were about ten of us to serve him, both male and female. If we went on a tour outside the Citadel, like a picnic, I was responsible for bringing different sorts of things. We traveled in French cars during the French times—Peugeots and Citroëns. The emperor knew how to drive, but he never did it himself. I remember once we went up to the hills to hunt wild elephants. Bao Dai also liked to fish and hunt deer. He rode horses and played tennis, too. Other emperors had very limited lives, but Bao Dai lived half in the West and half in the East."

His wife has quite distinct memories of the French period, when the emperor was little more than a puppet of the colonial regime. "I came to work for the royal family in 1937," she says proudly. "That's when the French dominated here. They ran all our affairs, and Bao Dai had nothing better to do than eat and play and entertain himself in different ways. He really didn't have any power. You must understand what it's like in a colonized country."

One of the remarkable things about the Phams is their obvious fondness for members of the royal family. Their living room is adorned with portraits of imperial figures. Especially prominent were the old photos of Bao Dai: the teenage emperor in a French military outfit; posing with Ho Chi Minh and an American general on the eve of his abdication.

In her capacity as a cook, Nguyen was responsible for preparing what must have been some of the most lavish meals in Vietnamese history. She learned from the previous generation of royal chefs, who had fed Bao Dai's predecessors in the Purple Palace. Fresh ingredients were culled from the local market, but prepared in ways that made them distinct from the dishes eaten by mere mortals. The emperor ate alone in his private compartment; his family dined together in a separate room.

The Phams were expelled from the Citadel with the rest of the imperial household in the early 1950s and spent two decades wandering through South Vietnam in pursuit of odd jobs. In 1972, on the eve of the American withdrawal, they went to work for Doan Huy, Bao Dai's aging mother, and moved into the house in which they live today.

Doan Huy had purchased the villa in 1954 after her son went into exile and she herself was ignominiously forced from the Citadel. During the Tet Offensive, the South Vietnamese government offered to helicopter her to safety, but the old lady refused to budge, electing to sit out the battle in the comfort of her own home. Bullet holes scar the palm trees in the garden, testament to the fierce fighting waged around the house. An irascible and stubborn old lady, Doan Huy lived here until her death in 1980, although by that time the property had been seized by the state. The Phams are allowed to stay on as official caretakers of the royal legacy; once they die, the house will become a museum.

The villa is not so much a place of the living but a shrine to the dead, a memorial to past members of the royal family. In the dining room is a huge altar dedicated to Doan Huy herself. An upstairs bedroom has been converted into an imperial tabernacle: three gilt buddhas repose atop a wooden altar, surrounded by faded black-and-white photos of Bao Dai, his father (the flamboyant Khai Dinh), and his paternal and maternal grandmothers. The walls and ceiling are charred black from incense. Burning joss sticks and plates of fruit sit before the altar. Across the hall, in the Phams' bedroom, sits a 440-pound copper statue of the fourteen-year-old Bao Dai, and a bronze bust of the "last emperor" rests atop a wooden chest of drawers.

Nguyen removes a sheet of paper from a box and holds it up to the light. "This is Bao Dai's last letter to his mother," she says. The message is dated November 7, 1980, and written in the rather detached, archaic Vietnamese favored by members of the royal family. It reads:

Dear Mother:

I hear that your body is not well mother. I am very worried. I pray to God to help you. My family in France . . . wishes mother well.

Your son,

Bao Dai

"Bao Dai was a very nice man," says Nguyen, speaking with a detached sentimentality. "He wasn't very active in politics or the military—not like Diem and Thieu. He studied in France." Then she

Patrons enjoy their morning tea and a smoke at a cafe in downtown Hue.

OPPOSITE TOP: Thich Tri Tuu (center), abbot of Linh Mu Pagoda on the outskirts of Hue, conducts a catechism lesson for three novice monks. The pagoda was built in 1844 on the site of an earlier shrine and dedicated to the Heavenly Goddess. Through French, American, and Communist eras, it has remained one of the primary seats of Buddhist learning in Vietnam.

OPPOSITE BOTTOM: The monks of Linh Mu ring this giant bell before prayers at seven in the morning and four in the afternoon each day. The bell, cast in 1710, weighs more than 7,000 pounds and can be heard more than seven miles away.

laughs, a witty gleam in her eyes. "But he wasn't as smart as his wife. She was very clever."

Hue is notorious for foul weather, often compared to summer in San Francisco. Almost every guidebook recommends an umbrella or raincoat, warning of gray skies and precipitation throughout the year. June was supposed to be a wet month, yet we were blessed with a surfeit of sunshine and Rubenesque clouds painted on the pale blue sky. A cool breeze blew in off the South China Sea, dispelling the humidity that had dogged us along most of the coast, providing perfect weather for strolling the banks of the Perfume River.

The atmospheric conditions permeated the mood of the city. School was in recess, yet many students had chosen to stay in Hue for the summer. They gathered in cafés and in parks along the waterfront, playing cards, singing along with guitars, or simply talking and laughing amongst themselves. Few had enough money to drink beer; a pot of bitter green tea was a more affordable companion.

Across the river, the vast lawn between the outer walls of the Citadel and the Noon Gate provided an ideal venue for a local soccer tournament. I watched the championship game, a furious match between the municipal workers (in red) and the journalists (in blue). A cynic might say that the final score was analogous to real life in Vietnam: the bureaucrats prevailed by two to one. Trophies—and a demure handshake—were conferred by the reigning Miss Hue.

Beauty pageants were another sign of changing times. Previously they had been condemned by the Communist Party as a hideous byproduct of capitalism, a blatant exploitation of female workers. Yet now, almost overnight, they were encouraged as a legitimate expression of the grace and beauty of the Vietnamese female. All over Hue, young girls were shoving dogma into the closet and pulling out their long-forgotten silk gowns. A notion of candid beauty was beginning to return to a city that once thrived on the visual feast.

I stood gazing up a wide stone stairway at the graceful frame of Linh Mu, the Pagoda of the Heavenly Lady. This is Hue's most eminent Buddhist shrine, one of the most revered sights in all of Vietnam. The seven-story tower was completed in 1844, during the reign of Thieu Tri, but the site had been of religious importance for at least two hundred years prior to that. In a belfry at the rear of the pagoda

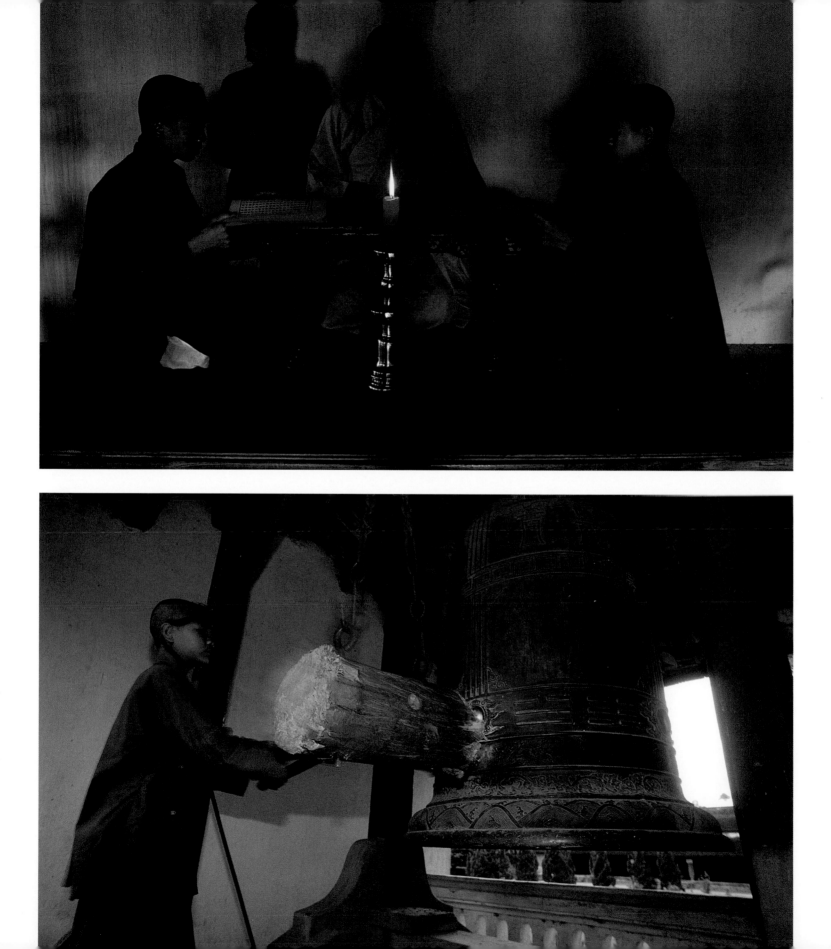

hangs a portly iron bell, said to weigh two tons, with a knell that can be heard more than seven miles away. It was cast in 1710, at least a half century before America's Liberty Bell.

Just then a loud American voice assaulted me from behind. "Hey, can you take my picture?" I was confronted by a smiling Asian face, a young man in a baseball cap, jeans, and white Reeboks. "Hi, where you from?" he asked in a thick Yankee accent. "All right," he enthused when I'd told him. "Another American. I'm from Spokane, Washington." Vigorously pumping my hand, he introduced me to the woman standing behind him. "This is my girl from Hue. Can you take our picture in front of the pagoda?" He spoke to her in Vietnamese, arranging the pose.

After the snap, the young man revealed that he was a returning Vietnamese. Born in Hue in the waning years of the war, he had left with his family seventeen years earlier and had not returned to his birthplace until now. "I have to admit that I felt a bit nervous at first," he said in a conspiratorial whisper. "But after two or three days there's no problem. Everything is cool." He gave me a thumbs up and trotted off with his girl into the inner sanctum of the pagoda.

Meanwhile, I had an appointment to meet the abbot of Linh Mu, a middle-aged monk by the name of Thich Tri Tuu. He was a shy man with a soothing demeanor, indistinguishable from the other monks in brown cassock and with shaven head. We sat around a wooden table in a cavernous room, morosely dark with great wooden timbers that supported the ceiling, lit only by thin rays of sunshine streaming through open doors on either end.

Tuu had first come to the pagoda thirty years earlier, at a time when Linh Mu and other Buddhist monasteries were becoming increasingly daring in their opposition to the corrupt (American-backed) Diem regime. The Buddhist movement's reaction reached its grisly apex in June 1963, when a group of Linh Mu monks drove to Saigon with the intention of staging the ultimate protest. Not far from the presidential palace, a monk named Thich Quang Duc sat in the street in the lotus position as the others drenched him with gasoline. Duc lit the match himself and burst into flames, the first of a series of self-immolations that sent shock waves around the globe. Madame Ngo Dinh Nhu, the president's sister-in-law and the most powerful woman in Vietnam, called Duc's dramatic death a "barbecue." She said "Let them burn and we shall clap our hands." Four months later

Diem was dead, assassinated in a CIA-inspired coup.

I was intrigued, and in a way mortified, that the man sitting across the table from me was one of the young monks who had poured gasoline over Duc. "We were not involved in politics as such," Tuu said in a nearly indecipherable soft voice. "But we Buddhist people always had the antiwar spirit. We supported peace and we demanded freedom for the Buddhist religion. By setting ourselves on fire, we were demanding peace, respect for human life, and freedom of religion—what we call real democracy."

He refused to be drawn into a discussion of how the Communist regime purged the monasteries after liberation. "Let's just say that the time before 1975 and the time after 1975 were two different periods. After 1975, the number of monks decreased. But daily life is much the same." He admitted that life had become easier in recent years: the Communist Party has partially relaxed its tough stance toward organized religion, and as a result the number of monks in Vietnam has reached nearly seven thousand. "Now that the government has a more open policy, we are not discouraged from speaking to foreigners. Before that, we were very afraid." The last serious confrontation with the Communists had come in 1982, when one of the elder monks at Linh Mu was banned and detained after writing an article critical of government policy. "He was sent to a reeducation camp," said Tuu, "but now he lives in America."

With politics relegated to a dusty corner, the monks of Linh Mu concentrate on the routines of everyday life. They wake at three o'clock each morning for a period of private meditation. "We sit on the bed and breath very naturally," said Tuu. "By that way, we induce only natural thinking. We concern ourselves with thinking about Buddhism, what we call the best things in human life. There is another phase where we question who we are." This is followed by a period of yoga and *tai chi* exercises in the garden. Morning is taken up by cleaning or repairing the various parts of the pagoda, or tending the extensive gardens. After a period of rest, afternoons are set aside for reading religious texts or instructing novice monks, not just in Buddhism but in secular subjects such as science, languages, mathematics, and general philosophy. The evening is reserved for personal study or meditation, usually until late into the night.

"We train our monks how to avoid five things: money, power, women, rich foods, and sleep." Tuu felt obliged to expand on the last embargo. "According to the Buddhist point of view, a shorter time for sleep is better. If you sleep too much your mind becomes dull. And when you sleep you cannot control yourself. It leaves the mind free. I have many dreams when I sleep."

Near the end of the conversation, we were joined at the table by a young monk from a nearby monastery. He was learning English at one of the universities in Hue and, naturally, wanted to rehearse with a native English speaker.

"I want to ask you some personal questions," he said boldly, running the palm of a hand over his naked skull. They were really nothing scandalous: what was my job, was I married, did I have any kids? Then he asked me what I thought of the girls in Hue, those legendary beauties who have tempted men for centuries. I thought this an odd question coming from someone pledged to infinite celibacy. I couldn't resist turning the tables. What did a twenty-three-year-old Buddhist monk—with the same hormonal yearnings as any young man—think of the opposite sex? He blushed, holding a hand in front his mouth to disguise embarrassment. But he regained his composure and answered. "I think they are very beautiful," was his sober response, enigmatic not so much in his choice of words, but in the dreamy gaze that pervaded his callow face. I had to wonder what sort of fairies came to visit him at night. And suddenly I understood why monks avoid sleep.

THE TET OFFENSIVE

The Tet Offensive of 1968 was the largest single "battle" of the Vietnam War, although fighting took place at numerous locations from the Mekong Delta to the DMZ. It was a major turning point in the conflict for both sides.

The engagement kicked off on January 30—eve of the lunar new year festival called Tet—with simultaneous Viet Cong and North Vietnamese Army (NVA) attacks on military and government installations in the south. Previously both sides had observed an uneasy truce for the duration of the holiday, so the Americans and their allies were caught completely off guard.

Viet Cong forces reckoned that ordinary workers and peasants would immediately switch sides once the "puppet regime" had been eliminated. But they were wrong: the vast majority of southerners wanted nothing to do with the Communists. Certain urban enclaves were captured by the Viet Cong—including Cholon in Saigon—but the United States responded with surprising ferocity and managed to retake most of these areas in a matter of days. The one city where the enemy held out was Hue.

Hue was attacked on January 31 by NVA units that had sneaked down from the DMZ under the very noses of the American and South Vietnam (ARVN) armies. Within twenty-four hours, they were in control of most of the Citadel and the north bank of the Perfume River. ARVN forces were in disarray, pushed into one small corner of the Citadel. Meanwhile, Communist forces also attacked south of the river, overrunning local government buildings and surrounding the U.S. headquarters. In less than a week, Viet Cong hit teams rounded up and executed nearly six thousand people, most of them civilians they accused of collaboration with the "puppet regime" or with the Americans.

American and South Vietnamese troops counterattacked. Within ten days, the area south of the river was back in their control. But it took four weeks of bloody house-to-house fighting to liberate the north bank. The Imperial Palace and much of the Citadel were destroyed during the havoc, as howitzers and U.S. Navy ships pounded enemy positions in the city. Communist forces lost roughly eight thousand soldiers during the monthlong battle.

The Tet Offensive decimated Viet Cong military forces in the south. They never recovered from the brutal U.S. counterattacks and had to rely on North Vietnamese regulars for the remainder of the war. But America's war effort was irreparably damaged in a different way: the American public was horrified by television and newspaper coverage of Tet; antiwar sentiment surged; and the U.S. government began to realize for the first time that victory was more elusive than it had imagined.

CHINA

Elderly women hunt for clams in the surf along China Beach.

There is a distinct change of mood beyond Hue. At first you notice it in the headgear of the men, as the military pith helmets worn so proudly in the north retreat before an army of baseball caps emblazoned with middle-American associations: a farm supply outfit in Kansas, a service station in Georgia, or a junior college in California. How Vietnamese peasants obtain these caps one can only guess: as presents from friends and relatives in the States, or perhaps churned ·out by the thousands at textile mills in Saigon. No matter, they are prized possessions, a mark of distinction that southerners wear to set themselves apart from their stolid cousins in the north.

You notice a change on the highway, too. All the way down to the Mekong Delta, the roads become increasingly dominated by old American cars and trucks, rolling testimony to the fact that once upon a time Detroit made vehicles that could last, and last, and last. Candy-apple-red Ford Fairlane station wagons have been converted into a fleet of lumbering intercity taxis. GI jeeps are deployed for a variety of civilian duties: carting pigs to market, lugging ripe yellow mangoes, or whisking a jolly load of peasants home from a once-in-a-lifetime trip to the city. Old but feisty U.S. Army trucks, painted a fading olive green, moan beneath the strain of their age and the heavy burdens they must still shoulder: tropical logs or crushed stone or tons of cassava. And best of all, the vans, sixties-vintage Chevy vans treated with the same mixture of motherly care and macho esteem they would receive from a kid in suburban America. In some towns south of Hue you can pass entire blocks of auto body shops set aside for refurbishing old vans, where Vietnamese teenagers beat panels, buff chrome, and spray-paint the bodies in new exuberant colors.

There are places where time stands still in Vietnam, like this street in Hoi An that features an old Shell gas station and garage, and a former US military jeep now used as a crosscountry taxi.

Bougainvillea covers the facades of many of the old buildings in Hoi An.

Another legacy is Shell. Of course the original service stations went out of business with the fall of Saigon, but the name lives on as a generic term for pit stops all along the coast of bygone South Vietnam. Along the main street in Bien Hoa, at least a dozen stations call themselves Shell, each with a crude yellow-and-red "scallop" sign. But outside Quy Nhon you can find the real thing: an original Shell pump with a translucent bubble top, a true relic of the psychedelic sixties.

Blocking the route south from Hue is the romantic-sounding Pass of Clouds. For centuries it proved an effective barrier to Vietnamese expansion into the south and thus prolonged the life of the ancient Kingdom of Champa, cultural kin to the Khmer Empire of Angkor Wat. Even after the Vietnamese had pushed into the Mekong Delta, the Pass of Clouds often demarcated the political and social differences between the opposite poles of the country. Below the pass, a frontier attitude prevailed. The people were more boisterous, more willing to experiment, less set in their economic and cultural ways, more open to alien influence. The south is where the French claimed their first foothold in Indochina, the same region that so easily took to American might. And now pundits predict that the region below Hue will be the first part of Vietnam to prosper in the post-embargo world.

Our prelude to the Pass of Clouds was a brilliant turquoise lagoon, wedged between deep green mountains and a sandy spit of land with a fishing village. It was a glorious day, bright blue sky with a trace of wispy clouds. The fishermen were on the beach, mending their nets, getting ready to affix them to bamboo poles that would submerge in the lagoon at high tide. We climbed higher still, a slow and laborious ascent via a series of sharp switchbacks. Far below us and hugging the rocky coast was the course of the trans-Vietnam railroad, built by the French and still guarded by the ghosts of old French blockhouses. Weary long-distance cyclists pushed and panted their way up the incline, but farther along, one ingenious chap was holding tight to the back of a slow-moving truck that would take him up and over the pass. It wasn't until the summit that the Pass of Clouds lived up to its meteorological billing. Bus passengers crowded beneath the flimsy awning of a roadside café, huddled against the wind and cold. Beyond, thick mist swirled around the remains of a French fort and an American helicopter landing zone that guarded

Dragons decorate the gates of a Chinese
congregation hall in Hoi An.

Shredded cassava dries along a road in Quang Nam province south of Da Nang.

the pass during two forlorn wars. The driver wanted to stop for tea, but I urged him onward, to the warmth below.

A quick descent took us off the pass, along a lofty road of many twists and turns that seemed to hang in midair, devoid of any link to terra firma. We cleared a final barrier of clouds, and there before us was the wide aquamarine expanse of Da Nang Bay. Marking the outer boundary of the bay were a thin isthmus and a rocky promontory called Son Tra, an organic exclamation point set between fields of liquid blue. In the hazy distance, I could make out the open waters of the South China Sea.

Da Nang has been a fateful gateway for foreign visitors since the French landed an expeditionary force here in 1858 as the first step in their military conquest of Indochina. Little more than a century later, in March 1965, the first contingent of U.S. Marines hit the beach at Da Nang. The Americans built the largest runway in Southeast Asia here, an airfield that welcomed hundreds of thousands of GIs to Vietnam. They called the ocean side of the isthmus China Beach, site of one of the largest American "evac" hospitals and a popular rest and recreation spot for battle-weary GIs. In one of the manifold ironies of modern Vietnam, the government wants to convert the old air base into an international gateway for charter flights in anticipation of a rush of tourists roused by the popularity of the American television series *China Beach*.

This is certainly a place in need of an economic boost. Da Nang's population has risen by nearly half since the war, to over 350,000, and the city is said to have the highest unemployment rate in Vietnam. You see old women digging through trash heaps below the glare of street lights, and this is one of the few places in Vietnam where I saw children begging from strangers. Much of the downtown area is dilapidated, with crumbling villas and filthy streets, while the once-thriving port is now a depressing assemblage of rusted hulks. A city that has seen better days gropes blindly for a path into the future.

Perhaps foreigners will bring salvation again. They still seem drawn to the town, especially to China Beach, which at once represents both the exploitation of the past and the best chance for exploitation in future. Young backpackers pause in Da Nang on their sunshine tours of Southeast Asia; American vets search for the memories and little else; Japanese investors try to get a head start on the postembargo boom. And of course the Russians, mostly package tourists and diplomats, partake of a little sunshine and seafood before their return to the Rodina.

By the close of the 1980s, the Russians were encountering what the French and Americans had long ago endured: Vietnam's gradual disenchantment and disgust with the resident foreigner, combined with a repudiation of alien influence and a turning inward to traditional ideals. There is no better metaphor than China Beach. By now I was quite used to being called a *lienxo* (Russian), especially by children who couldn't tell one white face from another. It was always said in a bitter tone, but rarely with violence implied. But at China Beach the stakes had been raised: the kids kicked sand and threw stones as they uttered the term *lienxo*. That's why the Russians huddled in fleshy clusters, safe with their own, dreading not so much physical harm but the psychological trauma that comes from naked rejection. I felt for them in a way that only a fellow traveler can.

Throughout Vietnam I saw the waning influence of the former Soviet Union. There were plenty of Russian-made pressure cookers, clocks, and cars in the markets, but these were being overtaken by cheaper goods from China and more durable items from Japan and the West. Russian-built cars and trucks were evident on the roads, but I was told in Ho Chi Minh City that a used Japanese motorbike was worth nearly as much as a brand new Lada. By the early 1990s the bulk of Russian aid to Vietnam had been terminated as Moscow scrambled for solutions to its own severe economic woes. And the Kremlin had scaled back its naval force at Cam Ranh Bay, the only permanent Soviet base in southern Asia. Even the once pervasive Eastern Bloc presence in Hanoi had eroded, overwhelmed by the growing tide of Western businessmen and diplomats. The beleaguered Russian tourists of China Beach were among the last vestiges of but one more empire that had dared to come this way and failed.

It was another day on China Beach, on the verge of dusk. As the sun plunged behind Marble Mountain, I felt a tap on the shoulder. A Vietnamese boy, perhaps fifteen or sixteen, thrust a handful of dog tags into my face and asked if I wanted to buy. They were rusty, some of them bent, but you could still make out the writing. Bumgartner, USN, Presbyterian; Smith, USMC, Catholic. A flood of questions surged into my head. Who were these men? Were they dead or alive?

Hoi Van Pass north of Da Nang hugs tight between sheer coastal mountains and turquoise coves. The pass marks the traditional divide between central and southern Vietnam. From here south the country is decidedly tropical, with hotter, more humid weather and lusher vegetation.

Had they lost their dog tags? Merely given them away? Or had they been stripped from corpses along with weapons and clothing? I wanted to search for their names on that wedge of black obsidian sunk into the Mall in Washington, D.C. I wanted to know about Smith and Bumgartner, and the circuitous route by which their tags had reached this boy's hands.

Anger was my first reaction. I felt like admonishing the boy, lashing out at his insensitivity. How could he peddle such gruesome trophies? Did he have no respect for the dead? Then I looked at his face again and realized that he was too young to have even remembered the war. He was born around the time of liberation. These dog tags meant nothing to him, beyond a means of scraping a living off the random tourist. They could have just as easily been postcards or key chains. Impatient for a sale, the boy asked what I would pay. I politely declined and placed the dog tags back into his open palm. He skulked away, no doubt cursing me under his breath, utterly confused as to why I had taken such an intense interest in his merchandise and then refused to deal.

The MIA issue continues to smolder nearly two decades after cessation of battle. It remains a festering sore on the face of Vietnamese foreign policy, an interminable barrier to improving relations with the United States. Washington refuses to admit that all or any of the more than 2,270 MIAs are dead; there are many in America who swear that GIs are still being held in secluded prison camps; and a 1991 *Time* magazine poll revealed that fully 70 percent of the American public believes there are still U.S. troops being held against their will in Indochina. Even Vietnamese government officials confess off the record that it's possible (although highly unlikely) that a few GIs could have survived on their own since the war in some isolated highland or patch of rain forest. After all, Japanese troops were still walking out of the jungle more than twenty years after the end of World War II.

Yet the debate is not so much over the living, but over the dead. What happened to the remains? The Vietnamese claim it is an impossible task; that it's the nature of war that some bodies are never recovered—especially when much of the fighting takes place in impenetrable mountains and jungle. They count their own missing-in-action in the tens of thousands. Yet the U.S. government continues to insist that the remains of hundreds, perhaps thousands, of

American MIAs are being held covertly.

In an attempt to explain more than defend Washington's intransigence on the issue, a U.S. embassy official in Bangkok decided to tell me a disturbing story. In 1980, a Vietnamese pathologist fled to the United States. During his debriefing, he told intelligence experts that he had personally examined the remains of four hundred American MIAs in a warehouse north of Hanoi. U.S. officials didn't know whether to believe the man or not, so they devised a strategy to partially substantiate the story. During the next direct talks in Hanoi on the MIA issue, the head of the American delegation asked his Vietnamese counterpart if it was possible to visit a certain warehouse near Noi Bia Airport. Without explanation, the Vietnamese refused. Yet several months later, during the next round of talks in Hanoi, the Vietnamese insisted that the American delegate visit what was by now an empty warehouse. There was no way of knowing if MIA remains had ever been kept at this particular site, but the curious behavior of the Vietnamese led Washington to believe the pathologist.

Why would the Vietnamese government refuse to turn over the bodies? State Department officials say the most likely reason is that remains are seen as some sort of political bargaining chip in future negotiations with the United States. But again, this is merely conjecture. There's also the issue of "freelance" body snatchers, Vietnamese peasants who hide the bones of American dead in the vain hope they might receive substantial "finder's fees" from next of kin. Poverty tends to breed this sort of gruesome business, especially when rumors abound that certain American groups are offering millions of dollars for information leading to the successful recovery of MIA remains.

Da Nang was rife with rumors, the sort of street-corner intrigue that one expects to find in Indochina. In a closed political system, where foreign media are excluded and the domestic press heavily censored, rumors become the evening news, often the only source of information on certain topics. You pick and choose your rumors, tossing some aside as ludicrous while retaining others with a large pinch of salt. Two unsubstantiated stories were making the rounds of the backpackers in Da Nang. One was about two drunken American tourists who ran a Stars and Stripes up a flagpole in Dalat; the other

Early morning fishermen on Xuan Huong
Lake, which sits at the very heart of Dalat.
The local Vietnamese call this Sighing Lake
after the noise made by the wind rustling
the nearby pine trees.

concerned a young American woman arrested near A Luoi in an ill-fated attempt to find her MIA father. Both were meant to explain why foreigners were barred from visiting the Central Highlands, but in the end (as with most rumors) they aroused more questions than they answered.

It's one thing to listen to rumors, quite another to be directly affected by them. I had hoped to use Da Nang as a jumping off point for a major foray into the Central Highlands, using Highway Fourteen as a route to Kontum, Pleiku, and Ban Me Thuot. I applied for permission and submitted an itinerary to the Press Office in Hanoi, but I was told at the time that the highlands were a "sensitive area" off-limits to foreigners, especially journalists. The explanation was that personal safety could not be guaranteed because of Contra-style guerrillas operating against civilian and government targets in the Central Highlands, especially a group called FULRO (the United Front for the Liberation of Oppressed Races). The "oppressed races" in this case were the Montagnard hilltribe people who once had been close allies of American forces in Vietnam. Backed by funds and guns from both the CIA and South Vietnamese exiles trying to destabilize the Communist regime, they allegedly sneaked across the border from Laos on hit-and-run raids. We ran into a reporter from the *Washington Post* who had been given this same line. Much later, a Western diplomat told me that a British professor had been injured in a FULRO raid. Another rumor. It didn't help me get into the Central Highlands.

Yet equally plausible was a story circulating among foreign travelers and press that Hanoi had something to hide. No one could say exactly what, but that didn't stop people from speculating: they were hiding reeducation camps; they were keeping Amerasian kids at secret locations after moving them from the cities; they didn't want outsiders to witness the wholesale extermination of the Montagnards and the resettlement of ethnic Viet people on hilltribe lands. All rumors. None of them substantiated. And they didn't help get me into the Central Highlands.

Eventually, the government relented—just a bit. They allowed me to venture as far as the old French hill station at Dalat. I leapt at the chance, guessing quite rightly that it would be my lone chance to see a region reputed to be among the most beautiful in Indochina. After

a long drive up from the coast, I settled into a huge room with heavy wooden furniture and a canopied bed in a dilapidated French colonial gem called the Palace Hotel. I flung open the wooden window shutters and found myself gazing at a landscape more Alpine than Asian: a pastel church with a steep spire, gingerbread bungalows, and a lush carpet of pines that climbed up and over the hills that ring

OPPOSITE, CLOCKWISE FROM TOP LEFT:

Morning fog shrouds the old French villas and the steeple of the Catholic church in Dalat. The area was populated by hilltribe people when the French first ventured here in the 1890s. By the 1930s they had developed it into a summer retreat from the heat and humidity of coastal cities like Saigon and Da Nang.

A long staircase ascends from Xuan Huong Lake to the Dalat Palace Hotel, an Art Deco gem that once was the nucleus of French social life in the hill station. It started life as a royal hunting lodge in 1923 and was later converted into a hotel. The place has seen better days, but much of the original teak furniture remains, lending the Palace a somewhat seedy but romantic atmosphere.

Loaves of French bread and cheese for sale at Dalat market.

Dalat cowboys: they offer pony rides to tourists in the Valley of Love, so-called because of its popularity with Vietnamese honeymooners. The royal family once used the wooded slopes behind as a private hunting estate.

Bottles of strawberry syrup line the shelves of a shop in Dalat.

Su Nu Pagoda, a Buddhist nunnery in Dalat. Owing to its isolation and tranquility, the Dalat area has become a center for both Buddhist and Christian retreat, with numerous monasteries, convents, and seminaries.

LEFT: The thriving market in downtown Dalat comes alive after dark. Most of the shops are owned by ethnic Vietnamese, but hilltribe traders often sell their goods along the sidewalk.

Temperate crops thrive in the cool mountain air around Dalat. Among the local specialties are artichokes and strawberries, the latter made into a variety of products including syrup, preserves, candy, and brandy.

Dalat. I did everything one is supposed to do. I went up to the Valley of Love and watched the highland cowboys ride their scrawny ponies. I bought strawberry preserves to eat with morning toast at the Palace, and a packet of tea for breakfast back home. I walked the perimeter of the lake by moonlight, careful not to disturb the many lovers.

Most of the other guests at the Palace were Vietnamese, honeymoon couples and student groups. They would gather in the ballroom after dinner each night, spread themselves over the threadbare carpets or the overstuffed sofas, and watch the same video of Madonna giving a concert in Rome. Their attention hung on her every move, gyrations of the sort that need no translation.

There were a few other foreigners. Two Swiss gentlemen, who had dedicated their lives (and bank accounts) to the pursuit of old steam locomotives, were all excited, having come across a pair of vintage French engines in the disused railway station at Dalat. A portly American fellow with a video camera, who described himself as an "expat living in Saudi." He claimed to have spent six years "in country" during the Vietnam War working as a civilian communications expert for the U.S. government. My first tendency was not to believe him, but suspicion quickly vanished when I ascertained that he spoke impeccable Vietnamese.

The American told me he'd come to Dalat in the rather vain hope of finding a French planter and his wife he had known during the war, only to discover they had fled long ago. Their lavish bungalow was now occupied by several Vietnamese families. I joined him for a stroll through the thriving market in the center of Dalat, a walk that served to dredge up more long-buried memories. "Where are the Montagnards?" he snapped, coming to the unpleasant awareness that nothing was as he remembered it from the war." This used to be a Montagnard market." But I couldn't tell him. No one could. There was only rumor and innuendo to rely on. The only hard fact was Madonna in the ballroom after dinner each night. In that we could trust.

WELCOME TO VIETNAM

The first "official" unit of American troops dispatched to Vietnam was a battalion of U.S. Marines that hit the beach at Da Nang on March 8, 1965. Soon the once-sleepy seaside town was a gateway to thousands of GIs on their way to combat zones. The air base at Da Nang expanded to meet the inflow of troops until it boasted the longest runway in Southeast Asia.

During the war, Da Nang was headquarters of the II Corps Tactical Zone, home base for several Marine and Army infantry divisions, and the venue of Air Force and Marine air stations that supported troops in the nearby Central Highlands. The city also hosted the 95th Evacuation Hospital, the group of doctors and nurses depicted in the *China Beach* television series. Another distinction was the fact that Da Nang was one of only two "in-country" R&R centers (the other was Vung Tau, near Saigon), where war-weary GIs could take a break on the beach or in the bars until their next mission.

Marble Mountain on the south side of Da Nang was an infamous Viet Cong hideout, where during the war they hid in the maze of limestone caverns inside the mountain. At night they emerged with rockets and mortars to demolish scores of planes and helicopters at the adjacent Marine air base. One VC platoon operating out of Marble Mountain was comprised entirely of female guerrillas.

The highlands to the west and south of Da Nang were the scene of many fierce clashes. One of the most famous was the Battle of Hamburger Hill, which took place in May 1969 as part of the "Apache Snow" campaign to disrupt North Vietnamese Army (NVA) movements in the A Shau Valley. Troops of the 101st Airborne Division were choppered into the valley on May 10. A day later they stumbled into NVA units dug into the side of Ap Bia Mountain. A ten-day battle ensued, during which 241 U.S. soldiers were killed in one of the costliest battles of the entire war. The NVA eventually withdrew across the nearby border into Laos. But the victory was Pyrrhic: U.S. forces soon abandoned the mountain and it was back in enemy hands by June.

Later in the war, Dak To and Kontum were the scene of major combat between opposing Vietnamese armies. In April 1972, the NVA marched south in their first attempt to capture the Central Highlands following the departure of U.S. ground forces from Vietnam. They overran South Vietnamese (ARVN) positions at Rocket Ridge and Dak To, but were beaten back with U.S. air support when they tried to attack Kontum. It was perhaps the most significant ARVN victory of the war, stalling the Communist advance for another three years.

OF CHAMPA

A vast region to the south of Da Nang was once governed by a mysterious people called the Cham. Rather than tracing their ancestry to mainland Asia like the bulk of people in Indochina, the Chams are related to the Malayo-Polynesian people of Indonesia, Malaysia, and the Philippines. The roots of Cham culture go back more than a thousand years. At its height, the Kingdom of Champa was one of four powerful dynasties in Southeast Asia, a glittering contemporary of Angkor Wat in Cambodia, Sukhothai in northern Thailand, and Borobudur on the island of Java. It came under the sway of both Buddhist and Hindu culture at various times, a twin influence that can be seen in the Cham artifacts that survive. But the kingdom of Champa succumbed to Vietnamese aggression in the sixteenth century. The story is familiar, a fate that befell so many ancient civilizations. The Chams were more concerned with cultivating a higher degree of religion, art, architecture, and dance than in sustaining a powerful military force that could protect the frontiers. As a result, they fell victim to an inferior civilization with a vastly superior army. It was the start of a four-hundred-year period of gradual decline during which the Chams were attenuated by intermarriage and cultural merger with other ethnic groups.

Today there are about a hundred thousand Chams, only the twentieth largest ethnic group in Vietnam. Da Nang was once their capital; the entire coast down to Phan Thiet was their cultural heartland. But now their range has shrunk to scattered villages in Thuan Hai and Phu Khanh provinces. Even in these areas, it takes a trained eye to cull Chams from the ethnic Viets who comprise the majority population.

Detail from a stone frieze at the Cham Museum in Da Nang. Champa was a sophisticated Hindu kingdom that dominated the southern coast of Indochina from its foundation in the eighth century. For more than seven hundred years, it acted as a buffer between the Khmer Empire of Angkor Wat and the Vietnamese dynasties of the Red River valley. The Cham civilization crumbled beneath the force of Vietnamese invaders in the early 15th century.

OPPOSITE: The ancient city of Cham (see overleaf).

The ancient Cham city of Srisanabhadresvara (My Son) lies hidden amid the jungle of Quang Nam province, southwest of Da Nang. King Bhadravarman built this complex in the eighth century as a center of worship to Shiva, the Hindu god of creation and destruction. The valley was a Viet Cong stronghold during the war, and part of the ruins were destroyed in B-52 bomb raids. But fifteen temples remain intact, a striking memorial to the artistic glory of the Kingdom of Champa.

My attention was first drawn to the Chams by Dr. Le Ngoc Canh, vice director of the Institute of Folklore in Hanoi. The professor has dedicated his life to recording and eventually recreating the forms of ancient Cham civilization. "I want to restore their old style of festivals, I want to restore their old culture," he told me eagerly. "They are a very small minority, but very important because of their contribution to the history of this country."

Dr. Canh insisted on showing me a video on Cham dance that he'd made the year before, using black-and-white film that had the grainy quality and stark contrast of ethnic documentaries shot fifty or sixty years earlier. Sultry figures pranced across the screen to the beat of undulating tunes faintly reminiscent of Indian or Arab music. The first was a gorgeously graceful fan dance in which a half dozen young women created the image of a blooming flower. Then came an African-type drum dance with bongos and tambourines, in which the white pajama-clad drummers beat their chests and did somersaults. The third was a swaying pottery dance, filmed on a dark and brooding beach, the women clad in colorful knee-length tunics and with flowers behind their ears.

But the most exotic of all was saved for last, an overtly sensual dance in which the star attraction was an exquisite young woman in silk halter-top and shorts, baring more flesh than one normally sees in this part of Asia. Her adornments were topped off by a metallic headdress, floral earrings with tassels, and a thick golden necklace. The overall effect was stunning, a wondrous vision right out of a bygone age. She began her dance kneeling, swaying to and fro, gradually working up to a standing position. As the drums quickened, so did her muscles, her stomach rippling and arms rocking like some oriental version of a belly dancer. A pair of male dancers in skimpy loincloths joined her on the grassy stage. She looped in and out and around their sweaty bodies like a sleek serpent climbing a tree. The dance summoned up visions of Bali in the 1920s, the same blend of atavistic innocence and blatant eroticism that enraptured early European visitors to the Indonesian isle.

At once I could fathom the professor's fascination with the Chams. Their culture was diametrically opposite to the conservative, somewhat dour nature of Vietnamese society. You watched these magical dances and were immediately overcome. I found myself dreaming about the people who created these hauntingly beautiful dances more than four centuries ago. How unfortunate that now it is all gone. Dr. Canh had recreated (and exaggerated) the costumes for his film by studying *bas-reliefs* on Cham temples; the dances he had dredged from the memory of elder Chams or were imaginative reproductions of what was found in Cham art.

The only evidence of ancient Cham culture that remains plentiful is architecture, the remnants of fabulous cities that were built along the coast. Perhaps the most famous Cham site is at My Son, in an isolated corner of Duy Xuyen district, about forty miles southwest of Da Nang. I set out before dawn and reached the end of the paved road just as the sun was rising over the Cua Dai estuary. From there it was a hot, one-hour trek on foot through rice paddies, pastures, and eventually jungle to the overgrown ruins.

My Son flourished in the eighth and ninth centuries as a pilgrimage center under the patronage of King Bhadravarman. No one knows why the city was abandoned; perhaps there wasn't enough water to support a large population. Fifteen temples remain intact, more than at any other Cham site in Vietnam, and Hindu influence is pervasive. Although made from red brick, the temples, or towers, bear a striking resemblance to the "wedding-cake" architecture of Indian shrines, with a menagerie of decoration that includes smiling

Cham temples on the north bank of the Cay River at Nha Trang. The shrine, dedicated to the ancient Hindu goddess Po-Nagar, was built more than a thousand years ago when this entire coast was part of the powerful Kingdom of Champa. Members of the Cham minority group still worship here, but the temples are also a popular place of Buddhist pilgrimage owing to their reputation for curing horrible maladies and disease.

elephants and dancing lions, fluted columns that float on lotus-petal bases, and the ubiquitous chorus line of topless girls that seems to be the primary motif of ancient Cham art. The pantheon of gods is distinctly Hindu, too: Siva the destroyer, the wise elephant-headed Ganesh, and the fierce winged Garuda. Huge stone phallic symbols called "lingams" litter the site, although most have been knocked from their plinths.

Many of the gods are now headless, a sad testament to earlier visitors who whisked off trophies to private collections in Paris or New York. Yet the most serious damage was accomplished during the Vietnam War. My Son was controlled by the Viet Cong for the duration of the conflict. The U.S. Marines dubbed this area Dodge City because they invariably encountered shoot-outs on patrols in the jungle. American B-52 strikes destroyed nearly half of the ancient city, but Polish archaeologists spent most of the 1980s beating back the jungle and restoring a good portion of it. Nevertheless, much of My Son remains in ruins. "We don't know yet if we will leave the B-52 ruins or if we will rebuild," the caretaker told me, as he sat on the steps of a temple picking lice from his son's head. "The plans still exist in Paris from the original French archaeological survey. But the Polish team has gone home. The Indian ambassador to Vietnam came here a short time ago and promised twenty million dollars for restoration and upkeep. But no date has been fixed. I'm not very hopeful."

It wasn't until much later in the week, down around Phan Rang, that I came across living Chams. They were arrayed along the side of the highway, the men driving ox carts and the women tagging behind, balancing pots on their heads. They were just as Dr. Canh had described: rather dark people, with high noses and very bright black eyes, not unlike the Khmers. Just over the horizon was a Cham village called Van Lam. It looked prosperous compared to most Vietnamese villages, with tidy cinder-block homes recently finished or under construction. A village elder explained that there are about six thousand Chams in the cluster of villages comprising this particular commune. They grow rice, but also make a living from the sale of homemade ceramics and cotton cloth.

They lead an intriguing existence, particularly in their religious culture. Van Lam is divided into two distinct halves, one for

Muslims and the other for Hindu devotees called Balomans. It seems that somewhere back in their convoluted history, a good portion of the Chams were converted to Islam. The Hindus and Muslims lived side by side (and intermarried) for centuries—until modern religious intolerance struck. "In 1962, a number of young Muslim Chams went to the city to get more information on the outside world," the village elder explained. "They wanted to learn what they should be doing as proper Muslims. Some went overseas, to talk with religious leaders in Malaysia and Indonesia. They were told that they should not be living in the same communities as the Balomans. So when they returned, we moved apart. Now we worship Allah at our shrine and Balomans worship Hindu gods at another." Still, a remarkable religious harmony prevails, especially when you consider the travails of Hindus and Muslims in India. For example, the Balomans (being good Hindus) don't eat beef, but they raise cattle for their Muslim associates. Likewise, being followers of the Prophet, the Muslim Chams don't eat pork, but they rear pigs for their Hindu cousins.

One sad note was that the Cham language—based on the ancient Sanskrit alphabet—is gradually dying out. Most of the older people still speak the Cham language, but the children are learning Vietnamese in school. However, another ancient custom is still thriving: the Chams are one of the globe's few matriarchal societies. "I come from this village," one man related. "But when I got married I went to live with my wife. Women are very important in the Cham community. All religious and family matters are controlled by the mother. A Cham woman decides whom she wants to marry, and the man must obey."

The last queen of the Chams is still alive, ninety years old and living in a village near Phan Rang. Yet because she never married, she has no daughters to carry on the reign. When the present queen passes away, another institution of Cham civilization will die with her.

Quy Nhon lies at the southern end of Nghia Binh province, a modern metropolis in what used to be the heart of the Cham kingdom, a relatively young city (in Asian terms) that is still struggling to define itself—part fishing village and beach resort, part factory town and cultural node. Even longtime residents of Quy Nhon seem flustered in their attempts to interpret the city. "There's nothing special about

the accent," said one man. "No special foods. No special characteristics. It's an average place."

Harvesting rice in a small village in Nghia Binh province.

But Quy Nhon is anything but average—at least in the eyes of a foreign visitor with a taste for the absurd and the eccentric. This is the town of a thousand pool halls, where young men gather each evening beneath the glare of neon light to test their skills on the green baize table. Outside on the streets, capitalism flourishes in the guise of hundreds of shops dispensing Japanese, Chinese, and Thai consumer goods, most of them open until nine o'clock at night. I saw hundreds of teens roaming the streets in large herds, already slaves to Western pop fashion, wearing tight jeans, T-shirts, and white sneakers. They milled about on corners, ducked in and out of shops, or

infiltrated the dozens of snazzy sidewalk cafés in the waterfront district, places with low wicker chairs and colored neon strips that illuminated the youthful faces.

I stayed in a hotel on the beach, a sixties period piece with old American phones, a crazy psychedelic ceiling in the lobby, and Beatles songs blaring from a cassette deck in the bar. The seafood in the nearby restaurants was overpriced (for Vietnam) but delectable. Yet I seemed to spend most of my time in the central post office, trying to send a telex. I split my time between a book and the bureau's philatelic collection, which was encased in display cabinets on the walls. One group of stamps remains fixed in my mind: a wartime series dedicated to the American defeat. One showed a B-52 crashing in flames; another depicted a puny North Vietnamese soldier with a Kalashnikov rifle guarding a giant American POW clad in baggy pajamas. But the stamps were dusty and faded, perhaps neglected for years, the last vestiges of an era that Quy Nhon is eager to forget.

An hour's drive west of Quy Nhon, nestled in the valley of the Ha Giao River, is the rural district of Tay Son, one of the most revered places in Vietnam. In many respects, this modest farming community is a key to the national psyche—not so much for what happens now but for what transpired two hundred years ago, when Tay Son was the seed of a revolution that spread throughout the land.

Memories line the route to Tay Son. Poised on a hill to one side of the road are the remains of a French fort, the spitting image of a crusader castle with crenellated towers and a Gothic gateway. Farther on are the crumbling remains of a Roman Catholic church. But at the very end of the road is a new structure built in typical Soviet style, a museum dedicated to patriot Nguyen Hue. His story is known to every Vietnamese student, his saga a perpetual reminder of what can be attained against great odds.

In 1771, Nguyen Hue and his brothers led a peasant revolt against the corrupt local mandarin using a variation on the Trojan Horse theme. "He tricked the mandarin," said director Tao Quang An as he showed me around the museum. "Nguyen Hue pretended to surrender and was taken into the mandarin's compound in a bamboo cage. The people who brought him pretended to be loyal to the mandarin, but they were secretly part of Nguyen Hue's force. The

Huge fishing nets are often seen in the lagoons and shallows off the coast of south Vietnam. They are lowered into the water for several hours and then raised to trap fish and other marine creatures. This particular net is off Quy Nhon in Nghia Binh province.

rest of his fighters began to attack from outside, and they were soon joined by those within as they crushed the mandarin's army."

This initial victory matured into a nationwide peasant movement—simultaneous with the American War of Independence and more than a decade before the advent of the French Revolution. Hue eventually brought down both the Trinh lords in the north and the Nguyen dynasty in the south, reuniting Vietnam for the first time in more than two hundred years. In consolidating his victory, Nguyen Hue was also forced to defeat foreign mercenary forces, including a superior Siamese army in the Mekong Delta and a huge Chinese horde dispatched into the Red River valley by the Qing emperor. His most astounding achievements were the famous "Forty Day March" on Hanoi (1789) and the Battle of Rach Gam (1785) in which he routed fifty thousand enemy troops and three hundred war junks.

Nguyen Hue left more than a legacy of war. He codified law so that it would be applied equally to princes and paupers; he began a redistribution of land into the hands of the peasants; and he initiated a form of martial arts "boxing" that still flourishes in the Tay Son region.

Nguyen Hue may have borrowed from the ancient Greeks to attain his victories, but his downfall was cloaked in Greek tragedy. In the end, the Tay Son Revolt was an utter failure. Nguyen Hue died of natural causes in 1792 and his empire fell into disarray. His brothers failed in their attempt to thwart a French-aided invasion by Nguyen Anh, the ruler from the south they had earlier vanquished. After dispersing the Tay Son forces, Anh changed his name to Gia Long and became the first emperor of the Nguyen dynasty, the nominal rulers of Vietnam until 1954.

"We have an old saying," said Tao. "Gia Long brought with him snakes to kill the home chickens." Those snakes, of course, were the French.

Yet no one has forgotten what Nguyen Hue was able to accomplish. By using peasant troops and guerrilla tactics, Nguyen Hue set a standard for the Vietnamese fighting man. Although his movement eventually failed, it was an inspiration to later generations of Vietnamese who evoked the spirit—and tactics—of Tay Son to defeat the French and Americans. Some say that if the Americans had come here and studied Tay Son history, perhaps they would never have become involved in Vietnam.

Quy Nhon was the first place that I felt the magnetic pull of Saigon, as if something was tugging me southward to the bright lights of the big city. There was still a long path to travel, at least four hundred miles through three provinces. But a new gleam had come over the land: more lush and green, more obviously prosperous, less affected by war than places farther north.

The next city down the coast was Nha Trang, in many respects a carbon copy of Quy Nhon, a sleepy coastal town riding a crest of a minor economic boom based on escalating tourism and investment from overseas Vietnamese. The beach here is one of the best in Southeast Asia, a crescent-shaped wedge of white sand and turquoise water that stretches more than three miles from the port to the mouth of the River Cai. My hotel on the seafront was already spruced up for the postembargo boom with a fresh coat of paint, smartly appointed rooms, and flirtatious waitresses in the dining room. In fact, all of Nha Trang was eager for the anticipated rush of foreign tourists. Even the cyclo drivers were more gleeful than pushy, touting for business in a weird English they must have culled from the slang of American GIs: "Me number one. A-okay! Americans the best. No problem!"

But then again, the people of Nha Trang have long embraced foreigners with a gusto lacking in much of the rest of Vietnam.

Harvesting rice along Highway One in Phu Khanh province. Roadways are often used as temporary threshing platforms.

Peasants tend their rice fields along the coastal plain in Phu Khanh province.

Perhaps it's because their initial contact with the outside world was positive. The first Frenchman to reside here was Dr. Alexander Yersen, the humanitarian physician who is revered even today throughout much of Vietnam. Yersen studied in Paris under Louis Pasteur, then set sail for Indochina in 1885 with the intention of founding a Pasteur Institute of tropical medicine. More often than not, Yersen found himself tending to the everyday medical needs of the local people. Nha Trang means "white house" in Vietnamese, a name that derives from the white-washed villa in which Yersen lived. He worked here until his death in 1943 and is buried in a plot that belongs to the Pasteur Institute.

From Nha Trang it is an easy run down to Phan Thiet, along a smooth American-built ribbon of asphalt that remains in good condition for the simple reason that it was never bombed by the people who built it. The landscape changes dramatically from place to place. In Thuan Hai province, to the west of Phan Rang, the road threads a valley of prickly pear cactus very much like Mexico; and then farther along is vineyard country that could double for the south of France. Without warning, the highway crosses an invisible line and we were suddenly in the tropics, surrounded by a great expanse of dark-green mango trees in sandy soil.

In Phan Thiet at the southern end of the province, I took time to visit both a *nuoc mam* (fish sauce) factory—the foulest smelling place I've ever been—and a school where Ho Chi Minh had taught as a young man. The school museum boasted numerous artifacts: Ho's clothes and historic documents, his spectacles and manual typewriter, and the famous pith helmet he wore in so many photos. And of course there was Ho's bed. As surely as there are scores of places in America where George Washington spent the night, I was beginning to see a pattern of dozens of places in Vietnam where Uncle Ho allegedly slept.

Fifty miles from Saigon, the highway traverses a long straight avenue of rubber trees (Yersen brought the first rubber plants to Indochina) and fields thick with maize rather than the customary rice. Thirty-five miles out, traffic was starting to get heavy, the road clogged with private cars and motorbikes and ponderous country buses that required breakneck speed and death-defying tactics to pass.

The heavens opened and a tropical downpour commenced

A lone fishing boat makes its way down the Cay River on the outskirts of Nha Trang.

on the outskirts of Bien Hoa, the capital of Dong Nai province. This is a town of God-fearing Christians, for I counted a half dozen Catholic churches along the main street. These were not the decrepit places of worship seen elsewhere in Vietnam but immaculate chapels with fresh coats of paint and tidy gardens. The faithful, rushing to Mass, splashed through puddles beneath a phalanx of colorful umbrellas. Heathens (and, I suppose, diehard Communists) played soccer in the town square, oblivious to the rain.

Of course, Bien Hoa is known for things less peaceful. During the war, Long Binh on the west side of town was the biggest American base in Vietnam, in fact, the largest military installation on the planet. Fifty thousand troops and a fleet of thirty-five hundred helicopters were stationed here at any given time. Long Binh also housed a huge ammo dump, a supply depot, and a prison christened "LBJ" (Long Binh Jail) in a typical twist of GI humor.

The divided highway begins just beyond Bien Hoa, slicing through a corner of Song Be province and down to the muddy banks of the Saigon River. From the crest of a high bridge (another American relic) I snatched my first glimpse of one of Asia's legendary cities, the squat towers and lofty spires of old Saigon.

ALLIED FORCES

Although largely overshadowed by the American and South Vietnamese war effort, there were a number of other nations that contributed combat and support troops in Vietnam. They were known collectively as the Free World Military Forces, reaching a total of almost seventy thousand personnel in 1969.

By far the largest Free World force was from South Korea—dubbed ROKs, from the initials for Republic of Korea. At any one time there were fifty thousand Korean troops backing up U.S. operations in Vietnam, including infantry, artillery, reconnaissance, medical, and engineering divisions. Their primary responsibility was protecting installations along the central coast between Quy Nhon and Phan Rang, including the huge U.S. naval base at Cam Ranh Bay. The ROKs were considered tenacious fighters by their American counterparts, and GIs used to say that Cam Ranh Bay was the safest place in Vietnam because it was guarded by Korean troops. From 1966 to 1968, ROK troops took part in a series of ten "Maeng Ho" search-and-destroy operations in Dinh Binh province. More than forty-four hundred Koreans were killed in action during the war.

The second largest Free World group came from Thailand, which had as many as eleven thousand troops in-country during peak times. These included top-notch units such as the Black Panther Division and the Queen's Cobras. Many of the Thai troops were based in the Bien Hoa area, north of Saigon. Thailand lost 351 men in the course of battle.

The Australians also had a sizable presence along the central coast, numbering as many as seven thousand troops. Aussie pilots flew Canberra bombers out of Phan Rang air base to support Allied operations in the Central Highlands and interdict enemy supply lines along the Ho Chi Minh Trail. Meanwhile, a squadron of RAAF Caribou transports was based at Bien Hoa. Australian ground troops were concentrated at Ba Ria in what is now Dong Nai province, including infantry, armored, and air cavalry units. The Aussies lost 386 men in Vietnam.

Joining the "Down Under" troops were several thousand New Zealanders, including artillery, infantry, medical, and engineering units. They were also based to the southeast of Bien Hoa. The Kiwis lost 83 men in combat.

Much smaller contingents came from the Philippines, Taiwan, and Spain. Noncombat support was given by at least thirty-two countries, including NATO members Belgium, Britain, Canada, and Turkey; traditionally neutral nations such as Brazil, Ireland, and Venezuela; and from such unlikely quarters as Iran (then ruled by the shah).

I found it down a dark street near the Cholon Canal. The facade was dimly lit, hidden behind trees, like a neighborhood café that you might find in Paris. The doorman showed me where to park between a pair of black Mercedeses, then escorted me into the bar where I was met by the hostess. She was like a vision from a different age, a bygone time when this town was called Saigon. "What a dish"—that's what the GIs would have said. With long black hair and a guiltless smile, she wore a tight red jacket that reached just below the waistline of a black leather miniskirt. She said her name was Charlie, and she had a name tag to prove it. "Welcome to Le Mekong, please follow me."

Charlie led the way up a flight of wooden stairs into a cozy dining room on the second floor. It was like nothing I'd seen in Vietnam: crystal chandeliers and candlelight, linen tablecloths, and genuine silver settings—made in the USA, of course. The waiter was almost as smart as Charlie, in his starched white shirt and black bow tie. He handed over the menu and wine list, clicking his heels as he paced away. French food and wine was the specialty of the house. The chef had been trained in Paris. What more could we ask for? A little music, perhaps. Two young men with violin and guitar were just setting up in the corner for a duet. Like most everything at Le Mekong, their repertoire hailed from a distant shore, European classics and old American folk tunes. After a few sips of wine, you could lean back in your chair, squint your eyes, and travel back in time.

This is Ho Chi Minh City gliding into the nineties. It's not like it used to be. On the other hand, it's an awful lot like it was before that. If

The view down Tran Hung Avenue in Cholon, the bustling Chinese section of Ho Chi Minh City. The name means "Great Market," and that in effect is what Cholon is: an around-the-clock emporium of consumer goods ranging from soap to color television sets. At the end of the street is St. Francis Church, where President Diem and his brother were assassinated in 1963 as part of an American-backed military coup.

Saturday night in the city. The old Continental Hotel on the north side of the square is where Somerset Maugham and Graham Greene stayed during their visits to Saigon.

New car and bar on Dong Khoi Street. Vietnamese refugees in America and France have already started to invest heavily in the old country, but big-league investors await the end of the American economic embargo.

Motorbikes and blue jeans are the status symbols of youth, like just about everywhere else on the planet. But Saigonese girls add that extra touch of class: pink elbow-length gloves to protect themselves from the sun.

French bread and pâté have always been popular in Ho Chi Minh City, but now there's competition from a new breed of fast-food joints that dispense "Caliphonia" burgers.

Maxime's has been the city's number one nightspot for as long as anyone can remember. The elite of colonial society flocked here for French haute cuisine and supperclub entertainment. The club now caters to the emerging merchant middle class of Ho Chi Minh City.

Ho Chi Minh looks down on the main lobby of the Central Post Office in the city that now bears his name.

New Year's Eve dance at the Cuu Long Hotel. Rock 'n' roll still captures the imagination of young urban Vietnamese.

Saigon artist Diep Minh Chau is one of the more renowned sculptors in Vietnam. While public art continued to flourish under the patronage of the Communist government, private galleries have only begun to appear again since the introduction of *doi moi* in the late 1980s.

Hundreds of people trek to the banks of the Saigon River each morning for *tai chi*.

Rue Catinat was a street of trendy cafés and boutiques in French colonial days. After years of government-imposed austerity, a bit of the old chic is beginning to return, although these days the thoroughfare is called Dong Khoi (Simultaneous Uprising) Street.

that sounds like doubletalk, then consider the history of this oft-maligned town. Before liberation, old Saigon was one of the rough and tumble cities of Asia, wide open in every sense of the term. This was R&R central for American GIs. They could get anything here: booze, dope, and as many girls as they could pay for—which was a lot, since they were cheap. The streets were choked with motorbikes and automobiles, the shops were overflowing with the latest Western goods. Fortunes could be made and lost in a day on the black market. And life was cheap. Russian roulette was no Hollywood fan-tasy.

Then came the fall. April 1975. To the victors went the spoils. But the Communists didn't know what to do with a thriving, vice-ridden, capitalist *entrepôt*. So they shut it down. Cleaned out the hookers and the hucksters. Scoured the place until it was squeaky clean. Until the economy had ground to a halt. Until there wasn't an ounce of personality. They even changed the name to Ho Chi Minh City, after the great revolutionary leader. It didn't matter that the people of Saigon refused to call it anything but its old, familiar name. The sterility endured for about fifteen years, until *doi moi*—"renovation"—followed on the heels of *perestroika* in Russia. Ho Chi Minh City was first to take up the challenge of free-market economics. The mercantile instinct had never faded, and like a great bear awakening after a long winter's sleep, capitalism re-emerged with full-blown fury.

Ho Chi Minh City would love to become the new Bangkok of Southeast Asia. The shops are packed to the rafters with consumer goods, as local merchants make fortunes off everything from color TVs to Super Mario games. Hong Bang Avenue in Cholon is a great bazaar, block after block of consumer electronic shops, with people hustling and bustling below the glare of neon tubes. Closer in to the city center, Ben Thanh Market presents a helter-skelter assortment of goods from around the globe: Seiko watches and Sony Walkmans, Ivory soap and Palmolive shampoo, jeans from Thailand and cheap cottons from China. On almost every street corner you can buy cigarettes or lottery tickets or get your bicycle fixed. At least a quarter of the city's four million citizens are now small private entrepreneurs.

The government estimates that as much as 60 percent of the goods for sale in Ho Chi Minh City are illicit, smuggled from Thailand either in boats across the Gulf of Siam or via the long and arduous land route through Cambodia. The authorities call the black

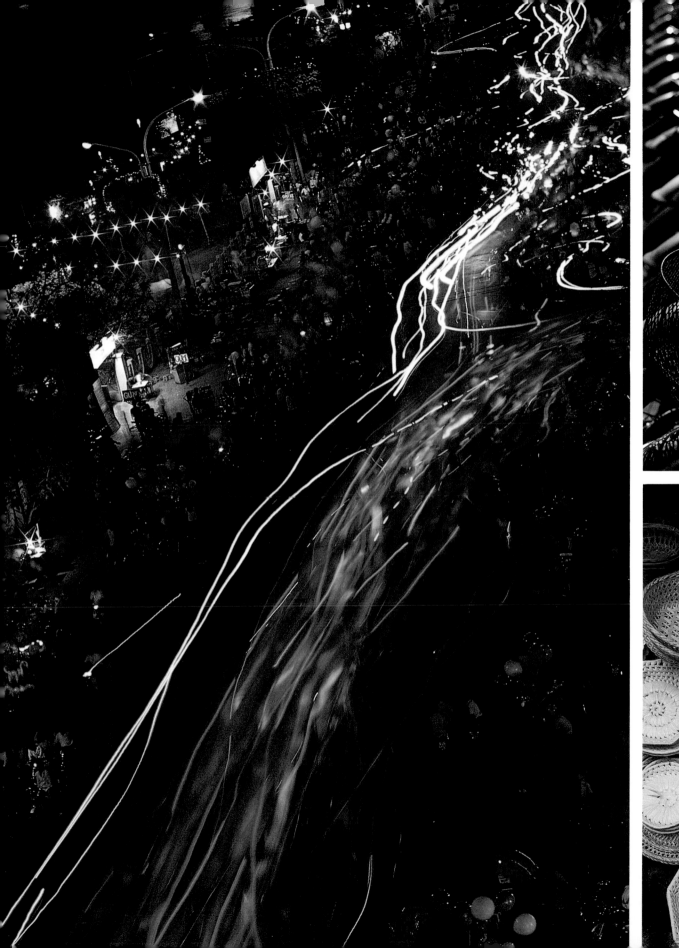

CLOCKWISE FROM TOP LEFT: Images of American pop star Madonna adorn a sidewalk stall in the middle of Ho Chi Minh City. After two decades of isolation, the Vietnamese have a thirst for almost anything foreign.

Saigonese flock to Thang Avenue in Cholon to purchase color televisions, video recorders, and stereo systems. Japanese and South Korean electronic goods crowd the sidewalks, although many of the goods are still beyond the economic reach of the average Vietnamese worker.

Gourmet street food: baguettes, French cheese, and Thai sardines.

Once shunned as capitalist cuisine, French fare like frogs legs and chateaubriand have returned. Economic reforms spurred the opening of dozens of new restaurants in Ho Chi Minh City, patronized by a growing number of tourists, business visitors, and the new urban elite.

market a "phony" economy. And in many ways it is, driving up inflation and making local currency worthless. "We will stop it," one official told me, "but it takes time." Hanoi had already banned the sale of foreign cigarettes and was considering similar bans on other products, as a partial means of thwarting the black marketeers. Recently Ho Chi Minh City police had arrested a "millionaire smuggler" and confiscated his property: four villas, seven foreign vehicles, four fishing trawlers, $1 million in cash, and over a hundred pounds of gold worth more than $6.5 million.

In a further move to combat the black market, both the central and civic governments are trying to create a "real" economy based on manufacturing, raw materials, and services. It's a bit slow off the mark, but there are encouraging signs in many quarters. The manufacturing base in the south has expanded rapidly. Almost anything stamped with "MADE IN VIETNAM"—packaged foods, drinks, toiletry items, garments—is actually made in Ho Chi Minh City. Most of the Japanese conglomerates have established subsidiary offices here, not to export what Vietnam currently produces, but to have a foot in the door for setting up factories and assembly plants once the U.S. embargo ends. Meanwhile, the government is developing a special economic zone in suburban Ho Chi Minh City to attract foreign

ABOVE LEFT: Lottery tickets for sale on the streets of Ho Chi Minh City. Residents spend millions of dong on tickets, hoping to become the lucky winner of a new motorbike, VCR, or camcorder.

ABOVE RIGHT: A guitar man hawks plastic-wrapped instruments on the streets of Ho Chi Minh City.

Middle Beach, Vung Tau.

joint-venture partners in the fields of light industry and electronic component assembly.

The service industry changes daily, as entrepreneurs scramble to take advantage of the sudden increase in wealth. Nightclubs and restaurants are flourishing once again; massage parlors and street-walkers have come out of their long hibernation. The Visa card started its indefatigable march across Vietnam (although Americans can't use it there) with the opening of the country's first credit card processing facility—the Saigon Datacard Center—in 1990. That same year, Ogilvy & Mather became the first Western advertising agency to set up shop in Vietnam, a "working relationship" with local partners called Saigon Advertising.

Perhaps the most impressive example of things to come is the Saigon Floating Hotel, the country's first modern hotel, and one of its few wholly owned foreign enterprises. The hotel's arrival was one of the events of the century. Thousands of people lined the banks of the Saigon River as it was towed into place. "You know that scene from *Close Encounters*, where the space ship comes down? That's what it was like," says front office manager Craig McEvoy. People still come each day to gape at this marvelously modern contraption. If there was such a thing, the Floating Hotel would deserve a page to itself in the Vietnamese version of the *Guinness Book of Records*. It was the first business outlet of any kind to accept plastic money, the first hotel with international direct-dial telephones, the first with its own water filtration system. And it also boasts the only tennis court in Indochina certified for grand prix play.

But the biggest bonanza is probably oil, not in the city itself but in offshore deposits estimated at several billion barrels. Vung Tau, the old French customs port at the mouth of the Saigon River, has already bloomed into an oil industry coordination center. While America keeps at arm's length, her allies are stumbling over one another in a mad dash to secure drilling rights. The Japanese are planning a refinery; British Petroleum, Royal Dutch Shell, and Total of France have already inked joint-venture production agreements. Meanwhile, Vung Tau has also developed into a hip seaside resort for wealthy Saigonese who parade up and down the strand (actually three different beaches) in the latest Parisian trendy swimwear fashion.

Nguyen Xuan Oanh is a sterling example of the *nouveau* capitalist.

Since he is a former prime minister of South Vietnam, you would think he'd be a choice candidate for refugee status. But Oanh is one of those who stayed behind, who spurned life in the West to build a new Vietnam. After liberation, he became an advisor to the Communist Party and the National Assembly on economic matters. In 1990, he became managing director of the Investment & Management Consulting (IMC) Corporation, a quasi-government body charged with the task of luring large sums of foreign investment to the southern half of Vietnam.

"I don't know much about Marxism," he says with no shame. "A non-Marxist economist is what I call myself. Market-oriented kinds of management is what I deal with." He looks the part. Instead

Cargo ships at berth along the Saigon River, which wraps itself around the former capital of South Vietnam like the coils of a giant snake. The vessels bring consumer goods from around Asia and take back valuable Vietnamese commodities like timber, rice, and crude oil.

of the dour image presented by most Vietnamese officials, he sports a beefy frame inside a crisp gray suit. His English is impeccable, refined from a quarter century of living overseas. His whole style is different. Pugnacious as a Pittsburgh insurance salesman, he dispenses with the usual diplomatic shadow dancing and gets straight to the point.

"What are we interested in?" As Oanh repeats my question he leans forward in his chair in an aggressive stance. "Everything from A to Z. Investments in manufacturing of consumer goods such as household appliances, ready-made garments, agriculture, fisheries, tourism—just everything. We've had over one million dollars committed in the last two years. Most of that was in oil, but a third went into manufacturing. We've had quite a lot of bidders for office space, hotel, and condominium construction in Ho Chi Minh City. The majority of these people are from Western Europe and ASEAN [Southeast Asian] countries. But I've talked with potential Japanese and American investors, too."

The man is also a realist. He admits there's still a lot of groundwork to be done before Vietnam can successfully move from a controlled to a free-market economy. One of the biggest stumbling blocks to foreign investment is the banking and finance sector. Or rather, the lack of one. As was the case with Eastern Europe once the Berlin Wall came crumbling down, Vietnam finds itself with a shortage of trained financial experts. Cadres just can't do the job. In 1990—as America was dealing with the savings and loan debacle—Vietnam was shaken by its own banking scandals. A number of credit cooperatives collapsed, with dire results for the depositors, most of whom were peasants or workers who had invested their life savings in various schemes. The government blamed the failures on bad loans, bad management, and just plain fraud. "I'm not encouraged by recent events," Oanh laments. "Most fund-raising in Vietnam is carried out without much attention or consideration. The bank system is not prepared for it. There are few bank regulations—people can do whatever they want. We need to have the U.S. in here before any real work can be done."

Yet when it comes to the bottom line, Oanh is an unabashed optimist. "In ten or fifteen years we should be at the point of taking off. In the south it will go quickly. The infrastructure in the south is about forty years ahead of the north. It's not easy to offset the difference. It hasn't been easy trying to integrate the two parts into a unified country. The south is quite bold and courageous. Their mentality is free enterprise. Ho Chi Minh City is where the action is."

The woman has wads of U.S. bank notes in her luggage. Tens and twenties rolled into thick balls. It's difficult to tell how much. Fifty grand? Perhaps more. Yet the customs officer seems lackadaisical—as if she sees this sort of cash every day. Besides, there's something much more unusual at the next counter.

Another women has been caught with gold in her handbag. Not the massive ingots you sometimes see in banks but four golden rods, each about the size of a bread stick. A dozen customs officials gather around the table, intrigued by the woman's boldness in trying to smuggle gold into the country—no doubt to be sold on the black market. A man in a tidy green uniform produces a pair of scales and weighs each bar. Their total value is about eighty thousand dollars. That's a lot of wealth to carry around in a handbag. The details are carefully noted (in triplicate) on her customs declaration, effectively preventing the woman from selling her treasure to anyone other than an official government gold assayer—who will pay her only about a third of the street price.

These aren't drug smugglers or arms dealers trying to get funds into the country. They are mothers and daughters. Simple housewives. Driven by a devotion to share a portion of the good life with family still left in Vietnam—in most cases, relatives not seen in years. Those relatives are waiting patiently outside, faces pressed hard against the glass of the terminal lounge. When the woman with the wad of bills and her companion with the gold bars finally clear customs, there is uncontrolled emotion—tears and shouts of joy—as they reunite with their long-lost kin in the airport parking lot. This isn't the sort of action you expect to come across at a normal airport. But on the other hand, this isn't a normal airport—it's Tan Son Nhut.

Anyone who followed current events from 1962 to 1973 has the name etched on his mind. Tan Son Nhut was the first touchdown for thousands of American GIs, as well as the headquarters of the U.S. Military Assistance Command in Vietnam (MACV)—dubbed "Pentagon East"—and the Seventh Air Force. The field will forever be a symbol of the ignominious U.S. withdrawal from Vietnam. Even more than the U.S. Embassy compound, this was America's last

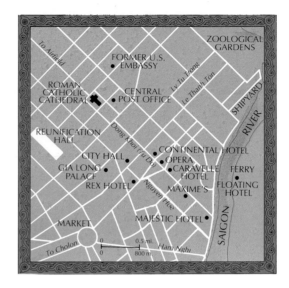

Ho Chi Minh City.

stand: where the last American casualties were suffered on April 27, 1973, a day before the evacuation of five thousand American citizens and Vietnamese "friendlies." How the world turns: Tan Son Nhut is again becoming the world's premier gateway to Vietnam.

Given the hardships of the postwar era—the chronic unemployment and political re-education and declining standard of living—it's not difficult to fathom why Saigonese now look back upon the "American Occupation" through rose-tinted glasses, a sort of nostalgic fondness that tends to block out the trepidation of twenty years of war. They remember there was an abundance of cash, food for everyone, and more private cars on the streets when the Yanks were here. But most of all, they remember the American days for their boundless sense of opportunity.

There are constant reminders of the "good old days"—America freeze-dried circa 1968. Lava lamps and loud rock in the disco at the Rex Hotel. A clothing boutique named after Snow White, with the Disney character painted on the sign. "Yesterday"—not some Muzak version but the Beatles original—playing as background in a government shop. There are less pleasant reminders too: the vendors who use old U.S. Army helmets as water basins, and the bicycle repairmen who store their tools in American ammo boxes.

Not surprisingly—given America's obsession with the topic—the most profound Yankee endowment is the motor vehicle. There are DeSoto buses and Jeep taxis; an old Dodge taxi parked in front of the airport; a 1966 Mustang convertible cruising Dong Khoi Street; "Cadillac" in huge letters painted on the facade of an old building on Nguyen Hue Avenue. The most brilliant tribute to the American automobile is a small lot on the canal side of Ben Chuong Street, opposite the old Hong Kong and Shanghai Bank, where at least a dozen classic cars are parked in a row. All fenders and fins like they used to build them in the 1950s—Dodges and Chevys and Fords—painted white or red, the engines purring like a litter of kittens. The mechanics have to keep the cars tuned because they're used nearly every day for funerals or weddings. It's so ironic that Vietnam is perhaps the only place in Asia where the American automobile is still considered the epitome of the posh limousine.

The dollar is still around, too, the currency of choice in Ho

Chi Minh City—and all of Vietnam. Downtown shops mark their prices both in Vietnamese dong and in dollars; you can settle bills with either currency. The same at hotels and restaurants—although some of them take *only* dollars. I walked into the Cyclo Bar at the Cuu Long Hotel, slapped a greenback on the counter and got change in dimes and quarters—coins minted in the 1960s and early 1970s.

But no one wants rubles. This is a constant source of bewilderment and frustration to Russian visitors. They come from a comparable closed economy, with prohibitions against the purchase of foreign exchange, which means they arrive for holidays in Vietnam with no viable spending money. As an alternative, they lug along plastic bags crammed with items considered scarce or expensive in Vietnam—shampoo, cosmetics, cheap watches, and the like. They peddle this merchandise to local hucksters who stalk the pavement in front of their hotels. Russian soap for Yankee dollars, which get recycled right back into the Vietnamese economy by way of a bottle of Mekhong whiskey or a can of Saigon Export beer.

It doesn't take long to feel comfortable in this city, or to appreciate its niche in the sphere of urban style. Despite the increased traffic in recent years, a bygone serenity prevails in the older part of town. There is an abundance of trees—avenues lined with tall conifers and leafy precincts surrounding many of the government buildings—perhaps more trees and open space than in any other Asian metropolis. Such a contrast to the city's crowded and jumbled cinematic image.

Best of all, there is a wealth of French colonial architecture, dazzling "tropical baroque" buildings in pastel hues that look as if they have been poached from the streets of Paris. Like their Parisian counterparts, they were designed by men with a flair for the dramatic who placed them at strategic intersections or at the terminus of long avenues, so that the elegant form of each structure is exposed and accentuated by its environment.

Notre Dame Cathedral reigns supreme over an entire block of the city center, with double silver spires that still dominate the skyline and fine brickwork that wouldn't look out of place in the old quarter of a European city. In the piazza outside is a statue of the Virgin Mary gazing serenely down Dong Khoi Street, seemingly oblivious to the carnality for which the street was known in the tumultuous days when it was called Tu Do Street and the rue Catinat.

Entrance to the Cuu Long (Nine Dragons) Hotel on the Saigon River waterfront. The building started its life as a French colonial abode called the Majestic Hotel. The Japanese Imperial Army used it as a barracks in World War II. During the American days, the hotel's Cyclo Bar was one of the more peaceful places in Saigon to have a drink; the antigrenade grills are still on the windows.

Just around the corner is the Hôtel de Ville (City Hall), clothed in yellow and white and adorned with ornate pillars and arches. It dominates the upper end of Nguyen Hue Avenue, peering majestically down on a bronze statue of Ho Chi Minh. Turn a quick corner onto Le Loi Street and you will come face to face with the old French Opera House. After independence it was converted into the Lower House of the South Vietnamese National Assembly, but it reverted to a theater once more with the fall of Saigon, an ornate showcase for Vietnamese music, dance, and drama, as well as for visiting foreign troupes (mostly from the Eastern Bloc). The old Post Office also survives, the forecourt now given over to a ragtag assembly of street vendors selling postcards, stamps, and their letter-writing skills.

Yet perhaps the most endearing colonial relics are the old French hotels. The sumptuously restored Continental, with an airy ground-floor café dominated by glass windows that look out onto the street. And the waterfront Majestic (Cuu Long), with the famous Cyclo Bar, where you can sit in a big wicker chair on the open terrace and listen to conversations swirling around you, as Graham Greene and Somerset Maugham once did, the tales of tourists, traders, and foreign correspondents.

What's remarkable is that this endowment of European-style architecture has been spared the wrecking ball, not destroyed in the name of progress as in so many of the former colonial cities of Southeast Asia. Rather than let these venerable buildings decay further, the city fathers are having them renovated and in some cases reconstructed according to the original plans, preserving the architectural heritage of Ho Chi Minh City for the benefit of future generations.

Philip Chow is trying to rescue another vestige of French colonial days. He wants to bring back big-time thoroughbred racing to Vietnam. Or more precisely, to the old French hippodrome in Cholon. Philip lives a comfortable life in Hong Kong now, but he's no stranger to this particular track. He was born and raised in what was then Saigon. His father and grandfather were breeders, and Philip was both a groom and an avid rider in his youth. The family emigrated from Vietnam in the early 1960s, and Philip eventually made his fortune in Hong Kong on Vietnamese restaurants and an

The Saigon Opera House is a popular venue for traditional Vietnamese theater, dance, and music, as well as touring groups from overseas, many of them from the Eastern Bloc. The French city fathers constructed the building as a municipal theater, but it was used from 1956 to 1975 as the lower house of the South Vietnamese Assembly.

OPPOSITE, TOP LEFT: Notre Dame Cathedral still dominates the skyline of old Saigon as it did in French colonial days. The church was consecrated in 1880, built from red bricks kilned at Marseilles in southern France. The marble figure of Our Lady in front of the right tower was sculpted in Italy. Hundreds of people attend Mass each morning, even more on Sunday when there is a full slate of services.

OPPOSITE BOTTOM LEFT: Bronze memorial to Ho Chi Minh, sculpted by local artist Diep Minh Chau and placed in front of the city hall in 1991.

OPPOSITE RIGHT: The old Hotel de Ville, former city hall of Saigon and now home to the People's City Committee, the administrative body that governs the Ho Chi Minh City metropolitan area. The building is one of the finest examples of French colonial architecture anywhere in Indochina.

Jockeys await their race in the dressing room behind the paddock at the Saigon Turf Club. As in Little League baseball in America, the youngsters must endure advice—and last-minute uniform adjustments—from anxious parents who want their kids to succeed.

import/export business. But he always had a hankering to return to his hometown and invest in some sort of project. Given his equine background, he thought the track was natural.

"I invested two hundred thousand dollars of my own money to restart horse racing here," he divulges as we take a seat in his "private box"—a row of simple folding chairs arranged along the top of a cement bench. However, securing the cash proved to be the easiest part of this escapade. Gambling was banned in Vietnam after liberation in 1975, so Philip had to convince the Ho Chi Minh City People's Committee to let him resurrect the track even though it was technically against the law. His gambit was government profit: he argued that citizens gambled illegally anyhow, beyond prying eyes, so why not allow racing and tax the winnings? It was an offer the People's Committee couldn't refuse. The first year was precarious, as Philip trod a minefield of abuse from critics who derided the "immorality" of gambling. The heat wasn't off until the National Assembly legalized racing in June 1990.

Philip isn't just the backer of the track; he's a breeder too, with seventeen horses of his own. "Yes, I'm, doing quite well," he says without pretense. "Making some money. Yesterday I had one winner and a second." All told, there are about seven hundred thoroughbreds in south Vietnam.

A day at the races is a bit different in Cholon. No strawberries in cream or mint juleps. The minimum wager is a thousand dong (about 15 cents) and the maximum five thousand dong. To win, you have to pick both the first- and second-place horses in a given race. "But there are no big winners," explains Philip, "because there are no odds. You couldn't bet a million dollars at fifty-to-one odds. There is a guaranteed percentage for the house." He estimates the daily turnover is seventy to eighty thousand dollars. As the key investor, he gets 8 percent of the take. The jockeys collect 10 percent, the owners get about a third. The rest goes into civic coffers.

A carnival atmosphere prevails, with lots of families and individuals who just come out to watch. People wolf down noodles or spring rolls at the cluster of hawker stalls near the paddock. Kids play soccer and basketball in the infield. There is a squad of paramilitary police—in green camouflage uniforms with automatic rifles—just in case the crowd gets out of hand. But this looks like a mellow group, much more fascinated by the spectacle than in running rampant through the betting booths. The amenities are mostly low-tech: the public address system sounds like a blizzard, the starting gate is operated by hand. The one submission to modern technology is a Japanese video camera set up at the finish line.

No one in the crowd gets excited until about fifteen minutes before post time. Jockeys gather in a dark room behind the paddock. None of them is older than fifteen. In fact, they're being coached and coaxed by their fathers, in a scene right out of Little League baseball. The boys look nervous and thoughtful as they await their race. Someone gives the signal and they march out to the paddock, mount their steeds, and parade around for the benefit of the punters. The horse are minute, mere ponies, their growth stunted by an insufficient diet and an inadequate genetic pool. Then they're off on the two kilometer oval—at least most of the horses. Some dally behind, kicking to high heaven, zigzagging back and fourth across the track. They eventually finish, sometimes more than half a mile behind the winner.

Four Western businessmen sitting behind me in the "private box" are loud and obnoxious, making fun of the track—especially the stewards on their rickety bicycles—because it's not as sophisticated as the ones back home. When Philip arrives they perk up and commend him on a job well done. One of them insists on being the first member of the Ho Chi Minh City Turf Club. "Only ten thousand dollars each," says Philip with a sly smile. The businessmen don't know whether to laugh. He just might be serious. You never know in Vietnam. People thought it was a joke when Philip first declared he was going to revive the old race track in Cholon.

Another remarkable thing about Ho Chi Minh City is the degree to which religion seems to flourish. I sought out members of various denominations, and every conversation was encouraging. No one claimed that there was complete religious freedom, but most clergy remarked that they were basically left alone as long as worship didn't overlap politics.

Buddhism has made a strong comeback in recent years. I spent more than an hour wandering through the recently restored Ba Pagoda in Cholon. Dedicated to the popular sea goddess Tin Hau, it was resplendent with all the accoutrements of worship usually found in a Chinese temple: huge brass pots for joss sticks, massive drums,

Hong Kong money has spurred the old French Hippodrome back to life as the newly christened Saigon Turf Club. A mix of serious punters and curious spectators converge at the track each Saturday afternoon for a slate of seven races. Wagers and winnings are modest by Western standards, but the average take exceeds $70,000, a vast fortune to any Vietnamese.

Christmas Day in Saigon: decorations in front of Notre Dame Cathedral.

and glazed clay figures imported centuries ago from China. Incense drifted through the main hall, where dozens of worshipers—many of them young adults—lit joss sticks or knelt in silent prayer. Another day, I visited the new Vinh Nghiem Pagoda in the suburbs, said to be the largest Buddhist complex in Vietnam. The huge bell here cost forty thousand dollars and was given to the monks by Japanese Buddhists. A religious ceremony was underway: a long procession of monks in saffron robes made its way through the temple grounds and up a flight of stairs into the main building, where the robed figures prostrated themselves and chanted before a thirty-foot-high golden Buddha. A young monk explained that this was a biannual gathering of monks from all over south Vietnam.

But more than anything else, Ho Chi Minh City is a stronghold of the Roman Catholic religion. More than six million Vietnamese adhere to the faith, the vast majority of them in the south. There are an estimated twenty-two hundred priests, most of them native Vietnamese. Wherever you venture in the city you see the spires of Catholic churches, nearly all of them well maintained and always with some sort of function going on, either a catechism class or a religious ceremony. At Notre Dame Cathedral, the mother church of Catholicism in Vietnam, Mass is said each morning and afternoon

Christmas lights adorn the facade of Notre Dame Cathedral on Christmas Eve.

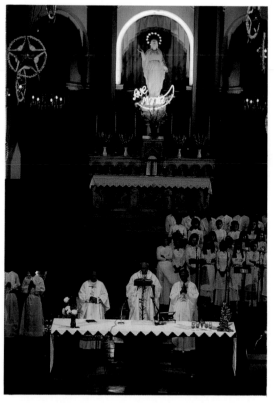

Midnight mass at Notre Dame: the archbishop of Saigon prays before a packed congregation of local Roman Catholics. Behind him is the Christmas choir, the women dressed in white *ao dais*.

and six times on Sunday. Throughout the day a small but steady stream of worshipers slips through the doors of the great Gothic building.

Christmas in particular is a joyous time for local Catholics. Most of the churches in Ho Chi Minh City are decorated with strings of colored lights, aluminum-foil stars, bunches of flowers, and Nativity scenes. Yuletide stalls selling special foods and gifts suddenly sprout in the plaza that surrounds the cathedral. The festival atmosphere reaches a crescendo on Christmas Eve, as thousands of Catholics take to the streets around the cathedral with balloons, confetti, and party hats made from Hero cigarette packets. Midnight Mass is a standing-room-only affair, as worshipers crowd into every nook and cranny of Notre Dame, most of the faithful dressed in their best clothes. The action continues until dawn along Dong Khoi Street, as youngsters zip up and down on their motorbikes and crowd into popular discos.

Even party cadres are not immune to the allure of the Catholic faith. I met a government worker, a card-carrying Communist, who confessed that he sometimes went on retreat to a seminary in Dalat in the Central Highlands, and that he sent his six-year-old son to a Catholic preschool run by nuns. "The school is officially illegal," he

TOP: What every teenage girl needs on Christmas Eve: a white dress, a festive hat, and a bag of confetti.

ABOVE: Thousands of young people pour into the streets of Ho Chi Minh City on Christmas Eve, many of them on motorbikes that whiz up and down the great avenues.

explained. "But the authorities look the other way. Later, when my son is older, he will go to a government school. But I will send him to catechism classes in the afternoon."

Yet friction remains between church and state. Although not nearly so serious as in the days following liberation, the harassment and arrest of Catholic priests and laymen continues in Vietnam. A government official from Hanoi told me, "The Catholics and the government have an understanding. They leave the Catholics alone as long as they are not involved in politics." He admitted there had been recent arrests. "But those are Catholics who crossed the line from religion into politics.

I also spoke with a parish priest about the intricacies of being a Catholic in a Communist country. "Before it was very hard," said Father John, choosing his words carefully. "In the old days, our followers didn't understand Communism. After fighting the church, the Communists no longer believe that we are a threat to the state. In recent years they are very quiet and they leave us alone." Then he added cryptically. "The people understand clearly and they see with their own eyes what is true."

Father John's main concern seemed to be lack of contact with the Vatican. The Communist government views Rome as a potential troublemaker in domestic affairs and has rebuffed repeated attempts to reestablish relations. "The Bishop of Da Nang had communication with the Vatican, but he died two years ago and hasn't been replaced," said the priest. Finance was another pressing matter. Vatican funding for the upkeep of churches and monasteries was also blocked. As a consequence, the church in Vietnam was forced to survive on donations from parish churches in America and France.

Still, Father John was optimistic. "Every year we have many conversions. After liberation, many Catholics moved to Ho Chi Minh City because they believe they have more liberty in the south. There are more younger people coming now, and they are very active."

She's not a holy person as such, but if there's one person who could rightly be called a "saint" it would be Dr. Duong Quynh Hoa. As head of the Center of Pediatrics and Public Health in Ho Chi Minh City, she has the unenviable task of treating the myriad war-related syndromes, tropical diseases, and general health problems that plague the country's children.

"For me, we are still at war," she says in English suffused with a stout French accent. "You don't see the war. But we still have an economy of war and a landscape of war. We also have the social problems of a country at war."

The most pressing of those social problems is chronic malnutrition, particularly among children. As Dr. Hoa explains, it's not so much a matter of famine—although there were severe food shortages toward the end of the 1980s—but the quality and quantity of food. With bumper rice crops available, people aren't hungry, but there simply isn't a balanced diet for them. She estimates that nearly 50 percent of Vietnamese children now suffer from malnutrition. As a result, the average weight and height of Vietnamese is falling in comparison to previous generations. In 1963, the average adult male weighed 132 pounds and was five feet, four inches tall; by 1990 that had fallen to 108 pounds and five feet, one inch. If physical growth is stunted, development of the brain is also impeded. "This is very dangerous, she says. "People are very slow; they must economize their energy."

Other pressing health problems are malaria, worms, and tuberculosis. These maladies could be largely prevented through immunization or medicine, but Dr. Hoa says that formal health

An entire room at the Gynecological and Maternity Hospital is filled with gruesome specimens of deformed infants. Although many observers jump to the conclusion that the deformities are caused by defoliants used by the U.S. military, the director of the hospital says there still isn't enough research to definitely link these birth defects directly to toxic chemicals.

After more than fifty years of continuous warfare, Vietnam has a disproportionate number of orphaned and handicapped children, like these children who live at a special home in Ho Chi Minh City.

Ho Chi Minh City has numerous rehabilitation clinics for war veterans. The vets make do with antiquated and often substandard equipment in their quest to become normal members of society.

care services are often unavailable in rural areas, particularly in the Central Highlands where disease is rife.

"The health problems of this country are very complex for me to explain, because they are not just medical. The government and the Ministry of Health are unable to produce enough medicines. For example, we are dependent on antibiotics from abroad. We lack everything in terms of medical equipment. And we have a lack of diagnosis and a lack of therapeutic medicine. One of the big problems is lack of hygiene. The most important thing is running water, but that is a very big problem in Vietnam. If you don't have running water, how can you tell people about hygiene? A second problem is garbage. You see it piling up in the streets. If you don't collect the garbage, it creates an environment for infectious disease. A third problem is latrines; many people use their local pond."

The thrust of her argument for better health care is that political decisions and poor economic planning contribute to social afflictions, which in turn foster health problems. "You achieve better health care by educating the parents and making them understand," she stresses. "But you cannot achieve better education without money. After liberation the government made many mistakes, particularly in economic policy. But the economic [domain] is always integrated into the social. As you see, now in Ho Chi Minh City we have a society of consumption, not production. If you want to advance in the future, you must have a society of production. However, to do this, you don't need resources but human potential. Perhaps now we have materials, but we have lost the human potential. We must start training the young again."

"It's also a problem of motivating the people," she complained, launching into a diatribe on the inequities of the Communist state. She went on to say that, in practice, Vietnam is a classless society. But in reality, there are two distinct groups: party members and the nonparty members. The cadres have a monopoly on powerful and well-paid jobs; their children are privy to the finer schools. "I think it is normal, it is human, but it is not right," she says of party privileges. "You must give all children a chance to succeed in this country, to become a citizen. If you always separate your society into two groups—the revolutionaries and the non-revolutionaries—you can never build your country."

Tran Bach Dang sits beneath an arbor in his garden, looking old and frail. His hair is ghostly white, his teeth are now capped in silver, and his voice is barely audible above the din of the traffic outside. He lives in a French villa that served as the official residence for the assistant U.S. ambassador to Vietnam during the war, a war that Tran remembers well. Until liberation in 1975, he was a mild-mannered South Vietnamese businessman. But that was just a shrewd cover. In reality, Tran was the first secretary of the Communist Party in Saigon. He was the master spy.

"I had a phony name. People knew me as the owner of a shipping company that carried products between Da Nang and Saigon. I didn't work directly with the Americans and the puppet government, but through middlemen. We even had business with American ambassador Ellsworth Bunker. My business role was not related to my Communist Party role. It was just for my protection, so that I could travel about without being searched. The police thought I was a very rich man, so they didn't bother me. In fact, I knew very little about running a business. I just pretended.

"At the same time, the Americans knew of the existence of Tran Bach Dang, the leader of the Communist Party. But they had no idea that I was living in the city, that I was the businessman; they thought I lived in the tunnels at Cu Chi. My photos were put up all around the city. The puppet government put a high price on my head, so I had to wear makeup to disguise myself. I also had a fat mustache. I wore a jacket and tie, and I had a fancy car. Still, it was very difficult. Sometimes I would have to stop at a police roadblock and I would see my picture on a nearby wall. But I knew that it didn't look like me, so I wasn't nervous."

He planned the celebrated attack on the U.S. embassy during the Tet Offensive of 1968. The assault itself was a notorious military failure: not one Viet Cong fighter breached the embassy compound. But the daring attack—combined with the overall shock of Tet—sent a stunning message to the American government and people: they were in over their heads in a conflict they didn't understand and had little chance of winning. It was a decisive turning point in the propaganda war. The Viet Cong had taken the American "hearts and minds" doctrine and turned it back against their enemy.

Tran now leads a much more sedate life. He advises the minister of the Interior on matters of "moral psychology" and is an advisor to General Secretary Nguyen Van Linh on political subjects. Yet there is another side to his life that is distinctly capitalistic. Tran is a budding video entrepreneur who buzzes around town in a chauffeur-driven Mercedes and is also the author of best-selling thrillers. Here's a spy writer who was actually a spy. "There are six parts to the series. It's based on the life of one of my colleagues who went undercover to work for the Diem family during the war. He was a captain in the puppet army and even trained in America. But he was really a Communist spy." He says of his books, "They quickly sold out and I got a good price," fully aware of the irony and not ashamed of the profits.

Another anachronism is known as Madame Dai's, or more properly La Bibliothèque, because the meals are served in the library. It may not be the best food in town, but it's certainly the most intriguing place to spend an evening. You imagine this as the sort of place where spies and soldiers of fortune and famous authors would eat. Credit the owner, Madame Dai herself, whose life reads something like romantic fiction. During republic days, she was a prominent Saigon lawyer (educated at the Sorbonne) and speaker of South Vietnam's Upper House of Assembly. Most of her family escaped to the West before the Communist takeover, but Madame Dai stayed behind to care for her disabled husband.

Unable to practice law and barred from politics, Madame Dai decided to support herself by opening a restaurant in her tree-shaded villa around the corner from Notre Dame. To dine at La Bibliothèque, one has to go in person in the afternoon to make a booking, so that the proprietor knows exactly how much food to pre-pare that night. When you return that evening, a servant shows you the way through the house to a musty-smelling library. The walls are lined floor to ceiling with French lawbooks. Various bits and bobs—family photos, ceramic pots, lacquerware vases—decorate thè remainder of the room in somewhat haphazard fashion. Madame Dai has managed to squeeze in six tables, each with a stark white tablecloth and a flower-laden vase. The restaurant is half full tonight.

To my right is a table of Australian journalists and their Vietnamese interpreter, engaged in hushed conversation. To my left are a couple of middle-aged American travel agents, who seem to be enjoying their bottle of French wine and the company of a pair of

Vietnamese girls draped in silk *ao dais* and with a trim of red lipstick and thick mascara. I have no doubts about how these women earn their living. Another freeze-frame: this could be a Saigon scene from late colonial days—the air of conspiracy, the smell of cheap perfume. *The Quiet American* come alive.

Madame Dai—in her seventies now, with her hair pulled back in a gray bun—makes the rounds of each table, chatting with her patrons in a combination of French and heavily accented English. She talks about whatever's on her mind: how hard it is these days to get shrimp for the kitchen; her childhood in Paris; her grown children in California and Canada—anything but politics. That's how she manages to stay open; La Bibliothèque is like religion in a way. When Madame Dai spots a customer eyeing a cat sprawled across a stack of lawbooks, she says: "Don't worry!. We don't eat cats here. You can count them when you come in and when you go out. The same number!"

In so many ways, Madame Dai is emblematic of the city as a whole: an aged European grace that blends easily with Asian exotic; a slightly melancholy air, but not at the expense of humor; and a passion to achieve something better, despite the myriad hardships of everyday life.

DREAM TOWN

The war effort was ultimately coordinated from behind desks in Saigon, the capital of the Republic of South Vietnam. The all-powerful U.S. Military Assistance Command Vietnam (MACV) had its headquarters here, at a huge complex next to Tan Son Nhut Airport. Among other units based here were the U.S. Seventh Air Force, the Army of the Republic of Vietnam (ARVN), and the South Vietnamese Air Force (VNAF). There were so many GIs in Vietnam by 1966 that the U.S. command decided to establish the huge bases at Bien Hoa and Long Binh as a way of reducing the massive American presence in the capital.

That didn't diminish the fact that Saigon was a GIs dream, the place where everybody wanted to spend his leave (assuming he couldn't get to Hong Kong or Bangkok). The American troops were famous for their slang, and to understand GI talk about Saigon a civilian would have needed a translator. Nothing was what it seemed. Saigon Tea wasn't made from leaves, it was the trooper's name for the watered-down cocktails served in local bars. And Saigon Rose was no flower but an allegedly incurable venereal disease you could pick up from Saigon hookers. Laotian Red wasn't a Communist but an alias for marijuana. Same with Delta Dust. The Continental Shelf was no geological feature but the brash rooftop bar at the Continental Hotel. And the Five O'Clock Follies was no floor show; it was the daily press briefing staged by the JUSPAO (Joint U.S. Public Affairs Office) at the Rex BOQ (Bachelor Officers Quarters).

Acronyms were a way of life. You listened to AFVN, the Armed Forces Radio Network Vietnam, where DJ Jean Leroy started each day with: "Good morning, Vietnam!" And you never gave the time of day to an REMF—a "rear echelon motherfucker"—a military desk jockey who never fought anything more dangerous than the traffic in downtown Saigon. One Hundred Pee Alley was a seedy red-light district outside the gates of Tan Son Nhut air base. Soul City was Saigon's fourth district, where the bars were reserved for black GIs. The White Mice were the corrupt Saigon Police (the name derived from their white uniforms).

Saigon didn't see much combat. There were a number of Viet Cong terrorist attacks in the mid 1960s, like the famous car bomb attack on the old U.S. embassy and the sinking of the USS Card in the Saigon River. But the only serious fighting came during the Tet Offensive of 1968, when the Viet Cong briefly captured Cholon and staged a daring attack on the new U.S. embassy compound (although they never got beyond the gates). Perhaps wartime Saigon will always be remembered for the photograph of that last flight out: a CIA chopper lifting off the roof of the U.S. embassy.

KAMPUCHEA
(CAMBODIA)

Mekong R.

TAY NINH

TAY NINH

SONG BE

Saigon R. DONG NAI

HO CHI MINH CITY
(SAIGON)

Phu Chau

Chau Doc

DONG THAP

LONG AN

AN GIANG

TIEN GIANG

LONG XUYEN

MY THO

VUNG TAO

Hon Dat

VINH
LONG

BEN TRE

BEN TRE

CAN THO

RACH GIA

CUU LONG

MEKONG DELTA

Phung Hiep

KIEN GIANG

HAU GIANG

SOC TRANG

BAC LIEU

MINH HAI

CA MAU

N

SOUTH CHINA SEA

| 0 | | 50 mi. |
| 0 | | 80 km. |

Deltas tend to be mysterious places, impenetrable coalitions of swamp, forest, and glade that subjugate the mouths of great rivers. Land and water are fluctuating commodities, vulnerable to the whims and fancies of the current. Channels meander back and forth; islands come and go; clumps of vegetation become floating islands in their own right. Well supplied with dangerous animals and strange maladies for which there are no cures, deltas resist human habitation. Difficult to breach and impossible to tame, they are miscreant lands beyond frontiers of civilization, places where only the most daring (or desperate) will venture. Indeed, people who inhabit deltas are a special breed. By nature they are cautious, leaning toward xenophobia, obsessed with introspection. After all, they came to the delta for a reason—to get away from the prying eyes of the outside world. They create their own peculiar, insular societies within the labyrinth of land and water.

There is no better example of this murky legacy than the lower reaches of the Mekong. The river starts its journey on the Tibetan Plateau, winding twenty-six hundred miles through the heart of Southeast Asia on its journey to the South China Sea. Once it crosses from Cambodia into Vietnam, the river breaks up into nine distinct branches, known collectively as Cuu Long—the Nine Dragons—fanning into a delta that encompasses more than nine million acres.

The Mekong Delta was the last segment of the Indochina coast to be conquered and colonized by the Vietnamese. It wasn't until the early eighteenth century that the first permanent settlements started to appear. But lines of communication and transportation were tenuous,

Decorative details from the Holy See at Tay Ninh, the mother temple of the Cao Dai sect. Adhering to a blend of Buddhism, Christianity, and traditional Chinese tenets, the Cao Dai rose to power in the 1920s as a political, religious, and military force that was largely autonomous from the central government. Their most noteworthy symbol is the "all seeing" eye.

and much of the Delta remained beyond the sphere of central authority. It became a twilight zone for the castoffs of Vietnamese society: smugglers, political exiles, mutineers, and religious rebels, people who wished to camouflage their clandestine activities. In this way, the Mekong Delta gave birth to a wide array of religious cults and bizarre secret societies.

For many years, Long Xuyen in An Giang province was the lair of a mysterious and violent group called the Hoa Hao, a Buddhist sect founded in 1939 as a response to the peasant suffering caused by the decline in the economy of French Indochina during the Great Depression. The leader of the Hoa Hao was a self-proclaimed prophet named Huynh Phu So, known by his French detractors as the Mad Monk. He led a large and well-equipped army distinguished by their long beards and hair pulled back into buns. The French captured and imprisoned Huynh, but the sect continued to grow in both political and military influence. After independence, President Diem tried to crush the sect by exterminating its leaders, but he never fully succeeded. The Hoa Hao remained a powerful antiestablishment force until liberation. In fact, they resisted NVA troops long after the South Vietnamese army had capitulated.

Even more powerful was Cao Dai, a cult that claimed nearly two million adherents and its own private army at the height of the Vietnam War. Founded in the 1920s by a civil servant, Cao Dai traces its roots to Tay Ninh, a town on the northern fringe of the Mekong Delta. Early adherents built an ornate cathedral called the Holy See, which Graham Greene described as a "Walt Disney fantasia of the East." Cao Dai doctrine is equally bizarre, an exotic blend of three religions. Jesus, Buddha, and Confucius share equal billing in the pantheon of gods. Victor Hugo and Sun Yat Sen are among the blessed saints. But the sect's most pervasive symbol is the "all-seeing eye"—a concept borrowed from Tibetan Buddhism. Although greatly diminished in both power and numbers, the Cao Dai continue to worship at the Holy See, looked after by a pope and his female cardinals.

Cao Dai also developed a strong following on Con Phung island in the Delta proper, where a mystical leader called the Coconut Monk held sway over thousands of devotees. His epithet was said to derive from his habit of meditating at the top of a coconut palm. But his celebrity was based on a tough antiwar stance that often saw him

Ceremony at the Holy See in Tay Ninh. There are thought to be about two million members of the Cao Dai sect in Vietnam. Besides Buddha and Christ, the "saints" of the religion include 19th-century French author Victor Hugo, Chinese nationalist Dr. Sun Yat Sen, and former British prime minister Winston Churchill.

Another detail of the "all seeing" eye from the Holy See at Tay Ninh.

RIGHT: Clad in traditional white, Cao Dai devotees pray to the image of the "all seeing" eye at the Holy See.

Khmer child resting against a pillar at Ma Toc Pagoda.

at odds with the American-backed Saigon regime. Con Phung became a haven for American deserters, who found it one of the few places "in country" that was beyond the long arm of the military police. Although they weathered both the French and American periods, the Coconut Monk and his followers withered beneath the onslaught of Communism.

After liberation in 1975, the Mekong Delta lost much of its untamed mien. The religious sects put down their arms, and most of them faded away. Better roads, river transport, and communications made the isolated riverine communities more accessible to the outside world, more a part of the Vietnamese mainstream. With improved irrigation, access to fertilizers, and the introduction of hybrid strains, the Delta was transformed into the nation's rice bowl, an endless expanse of paddies tilled by Vietnam's wealthiest farmers. Still, much of the old mystery of the Mekong lingers. It takes more than a couple of decades to extinguish the force of a million years of nature.

It took a full day's driving and two ferries to reach Can Tho, the capital of Hau Giang province and the undisputed metropolis of the Delta region. The city sits at the junction of a small tributary and the Song Hau branch of the Mekong, about fifty miles upstream from the South China Sea. The river here is wide and slow, a living body of water that runs milky-brown during the rains of summer and crystal clear through the dry, hot winter. Commanding the waterfront are a silver statue of Ho Chi Minh and a rambling market that spills out from beneath its roof to encompass sampans, barges, and floating docks.

All the bounty of the Delta comes to market here: mangoes, bananas, pineapples, coconuts, mounds of rice, and a stinky green fruit called the durian; various sorts of fish and crustaceans; and live ducks, pigs, and chickens. Industry also revolves around farming and fishing, a factory for canning pineapples, another for freezing shrimp, and over a hundred rice-husking mills. Naturally, the university also specializes in agriculture, with a particular emphasis on rice.

"We are the belly of the country," said Phan Tan Tien. "We have the richest rice fields in Vietnam." As director of Agricultural Services for Hau Giang province, Phan is in a unique position to assess the government's new agriculture policies and provide a comprehensive overview of farming in the delta.

Phan continued: "We are growing a new type of rice that we developed in cooperation with a research station in the Philippines. It has a very high yield and it takes a shorter time to grow—just a hundred days compared to two hundred for the old variety—so we can also have more crops per year. Of course, there are problems with the new rice. The plants are very short: we can't plant them in deep water like the old plants or they will die. The quality of the old rice is better too. It smells better and it's nicer to eat. But we are always trying to improve—to achieve better smell and taste for the new rice so that it can be exported."

Not that exports are a problem. Since 1988, Vietnam has gone from a net rice importer to the world's third largest exporter. Rice exports doubled from 1989 to 1990, to a record two million tons. A phenomenal achievement by any standard. Hau Giang province alone exports more than four hundred thousand tons per year. The rebound of the rice industry is held aloft as a shining example of Vietnam's economic potential.

Phan attributes the turnabout to the liberalization of national agricultural policy, the decision to put production back into the hands of the peasants and to institute a free-market policy whereby farmers fix their own prices and sell to whomever they want.

"Starting in 1988, each peasant family was given an area to farm," Phan explained. "We kept the cooperatives to provide the peasants with seed, fertilizer, insecticide, and guidance, and to organize getting the crops to market. The peasants must now pay for their seed, fertilizer, et cetera, out of their profits. But they don't pay any income tax, just a land tax that depends on whether they are farming good or bad land. We have seven different land classifications. Peasants on the best land pay a tax of seven hundred kilos [fifteen hundred pounds] of rice per year to the provincial government, with half of it going to the national government in Hanoi. But this tax is never more than 10 percent of the total harvest. I would estimate that after taking away for tax and domestic use, the peasants can sell about 70 to 80 percent of their rice on the free market. Of course, they can also sell it to the state or use it as animal feed. It's now up to them."

Remnants of the co-op system remain in the north, where it

As "Uncle Ho" gazes joyfully at the Mekong River, farmers flock to the bustling market along the waterfront in Can Tho. The largest city in the delta region, Can Tho is also a center of agricultural research and education.

A fisherman repairs his net on the main canal through Phung Hiep. Although landlocked, the town is connected to other parts of the Mekong Delta by means of six navigable canals.

RIGHT AND OPPOSITE LEFT: Bumper-to-bumper boats form the floating market at Phung Hiep in Hau Giang province. The maze of waterways in the region functions much like a network of highways, allowing farmers to transport their crops to market with ease.

Black and yellow chicks for sale in
Phung Hiep market.

has proved difficult to break down more than thirty-five years of central control. But the co-ops disintegrated at once in the Mekong Delta, where farmers had fresh memories of the free-wheeling agrarian capitalist days of the past.

"In the old system, the peasants worked directly for the co-op and were called on to do certain tasks such as planting, harvesting, or weeding," said Phan. "But that was not good. The people became lazy and inactive. Now people have responsibility for their own land. If they grow good crops they have more benefits, but with bad crops they lose." However, that doesn't mean that social responsibility has been divorced from agricultural policy. "A rich farmer has much capital to invest back into his land. But a poor farmer has a shortage of both labor and investment. He is stuck with no progress. In the case of poor peasant families, the government decreases the land tax and provides long-term loans—at low interest rates—to buy farm supplies and seed. It's hard to balance. We just try to narrow the gap between rich and poor. But we must also distinguish between a poor farmer who is lazy and one who is just unlucky despite working hard."

So farmers are happy and production is booming. Now the Delta's other agrarian problems can be tackled. The most urgent is the lingering effect of chemicals used during the Vietnam War. It's estimated that more than half of the forest and fisheries in the Delta were somehow affected by defoliants like Agent Orange. Slowly but surely the Vietnamese are nurturing their environment back to health. In one pilot project in Minh Hai province, more than twenty thousand hectares of mangrove trees have been replanted—although it could be a century before all of the mangrove is healthy. And there's the down side of using chemical fertilizers and insecticides: widespread water pollution that poses an even greater threat to Mekong fisheries. "We estimate that in ten years, the fish yield will decrease by 8 to 10 percent from what it is today," said Phan. "This is only because of chemicals used for growing rice."

Dr. Tran Phuoc Duong is about as deep into rice as one can be—without standing in a paddy up to one's knees. As rector of Can Tho University, he guides the nation's leading agricultural research station. His greatest feat has been convincing American colleges and research institutes to work with their Vietnamese counterparts in

CLOCKWISE FROM TOP LEFT:

Bats swirl around Ma Toc Pagoda, a Khmer temple in the backwoods of Hau Giang province. With its peaked roof, circular stupa, and elaborate Thai-style decoration, the pagoda is in marked contrast to traditional Vietnamese Buddhist shrines.

A young rice harvester in Hau Giang province. The Mekong Delta is often called the "rice bowl" of Vietnam and for good reason: Hau Giang alone produces more than 1.5 million tons of rice each year, about a third of it for export.

Khmer children at Soc Trang.

Khmer monk at Ma Toc Pagoda. Small groups of ethnic Khmers have lived in the Mekong region of Vietnam since pre-colonial times. They were later joined by refugees fleeing the bloody Khmer Rouge regime in Cambodia in the 1970s.

Fish for sale at a rural market in Hau Giang province.

"Monkey bridges" span the waters of Phung Hiep, a busy market town at the center of Hau Giang province that is built around the star-shaped confluence of six canals.

Only the rusted sign remains of this Esso service station at My Tho on the Mekong River.

Coconut plantations along the Ham Luong River, a tributary of the Mekong that slices down the middle of Ben Tre province. The area is known for its delicious coconuts, eaten fresh or shredded for use in the local cuisine. Coconut oil is sometimes burned in lamps in the delta region, although its use is rapidly fading.

Sorting shrimp for export at the Minh Hai Sea Produce Corp.

The day begins early at Chau Doc in the Mekong Delta.

A time to work and a time to snooze: a *cyclo* driver naps at Long Xuyen, the capital of An Giang province in the western delta.

Bananas for sale at Bac Lieu market.

Mounds of delta rice for sale in the market at Rach Gia.

Khmer monks at Soc Soai Pagoda in Kien Giang province.

RIGHT: The temple at Soc Soai Pagoda is relatively new, consecrated in 1970, but two decades of terse tropical weather have endowed the complex with a bygone atmosphere.

developing new strains of rice and other agricultural innovations.

One of Dr. Duong's pet projects is biological nitrogen research that seeks ways to exploit natural protein in the soil, thereby lessening the dependence on chemical fertilizers that harm the environment. Soybeans are at the heart of the study because it's already known that they can enrich the nitrogen content of a field when rotated with rice crops. The University of Hawaii Nitrogen Lab has provided bacteria samples to develop organic nitrogen nodules; the University of Illinois has chipped in with research on soybean products such as tofu and soya milk; a university in Holland is providing financial support to develop ways for farmers to grow their own nitrogen nodules from soybean seeds.

"This is a very inexpensive way to produce nitrogen and avoid some pollution problems," said Dr. Duong in perfect, American-accented English. "It will improve the rice crop. But soybeans are also a cheap source of protein. And we need more sources of protein for the Vietnamese diet." He admits the toughest part of his job is getting old farmers to try new ways. "We have to prepare and make propaganda for the people to accept this. You have to sell the idea. Sometimes we have to give away products before farmers will try them. Farmers are very sensitive to new ideas. Many times they don't believe us. They say, 'There must be some trick if it's grown at the university.' But eventually they see for themselves, and in this way we succeed at distributing new ideas."

Educated at American universities during the 1960s, Dr. Duong is one of the few scientists who voluntarily stayed in Vietnam after liberation. Yet he never joined the Communist Party. As an outsider, he was forced to work for nearly two decades in the shadow of cadres controlling the education system. But in 1989 he broke the party monopoly on higher education when he was elected rector at Can Tho—the first non-Communist (and American-educated) head of a Vietnamese university. He oversees a school with five thousand regular and two thousand extension students, offering twenty-three types of degrees in agriculture, medicine, and education.

"Before, the head of schools had to be appointed by the central government," he explained. "He had to be a party member. Now he must be elected by a vote of the university community. I am still the only case [in Vietnam]. But at lower levels, they are now looking for people who can do the job—rather than ones who are loyal to the party. This is true in government and industry, too. Now they are looking for technocrats who can use their expertise for the good of the nation. This is a very important breakthrough. I think it will continue."

But he cautions that change must not be too quick: "Before there was anxiety and the future was very dim. But now people feel that life is getting a little bit better. I feel that way personally. The economy is okay now. Politically we are progressing. Not as much as people on the outside would like. But in Vietnam, we believe in moving more slowly so that we know what we are doing. At least now we see the light at the end of the tunnel."

At the end of many months of exploring Vietnam, I'd come to a few conclusions of my own. There was no getting away from the fact that Vietnam is a country beset by deep social and political problems. There is open discord between various factions that serves to limit national potential much more than the American embargo. Until the problems are overcome, development in all aspects of life will continue to move at a snail's pace.

Democracy is not just around the corner. Communism will gradually fade away rather then crumble quickly from within as in Eastern Europe. Neither is an economic boom at hand. Even in the postembargo world, it will take Vietnam decades to catch up with the economic "dragons" of Southeast Asia in terms of investment, infrastructure, and work-force sophistication. Poverty, poor health care, and education, the issue of state security versus personal freedom, and other societal ailments will continue to plague Vietnam in years to come.

Yet everywhere I traveled I saw signs of progress. Perhaps painfully slow progress, but forward movement all the same. There was optimism throughout the land, a confidence that had been lacking in ordinary citizens when I first ventured to Vietnam in the 1980s. People were beginning to look at the future with unequivocal hope. Most of all, they were pleased that the fighting was over, that years of conflict had finally been laid to rest. Peace for the first time in three generations. The Vietnamese had stopped thinking of themselves as a country at war. Now they were waiting for the rest of the world to do the same.

BROWN-WATER WAR

The Mekong Delta was a special place to fight, and it required special tactics. Laced with hundreds of small waterways and thick mangrove swamps, it was a perfect place for the Viet Cong to take refuge after their lightning attacks on urban targets. Among their favorite hideouts were the menacing U Minh Forest, Seven Mountains, and the Plain of Reeds.

The entire Delta fell under the framework of the U.S. military's IV Corps Tactical Zone, based at Can Tho on one of the northern tributaries of the Mekong River. Its primary means of enforcement was the Ninth Infantry Division, the only American outfit routinely deployed in the Delta region. Although it was a relatively minor engagement, the 1963 Battle of Ap Bac on the Plain of Reeds was a landmark in the history of the war. It was the earliest documented case of the Viet Cong standing their ground against U.S. helicopters, a brief skirmish in which they realized that choppers were vulnerable to small-arms fire. Over the course of the war, the VC shot down more than two thousand American helicopters.

With so much water, it was natural that the talents of the U.S. Navy should be required in the Delta. Task Force 117 was dispatched inland and dubbed the "Brown-Water Navy" after the primary color of the Mekong. From a base at My Tho, the task force ranged out across the Delta in heavily armed Monitor patrol boats on search-and-destroy missions against the Viet Cong. The Navy also combined forces with the U.S. Army to form the Mobile Riverine Force, a quick-moving strike group that could launch attacks with as many as five thousand troops.

Despite the firepower, U.S. forces found it difficult to dislodge the Communists from their wilderness outposts. They soon resorted to chemical defoliants. A large percentage of the 18.8 million gallons of herbicide dumped on Vietnam during Operation Ranch Hand (1962–70) was sprayed on the mangrove swamps of the Mekong Delta. Rather than their cumbersome laboratory names, the chemicals were known by the color of the stripes around their barrels: Agents Orange, White, and Blue.

VIETNAM TRAVEL GUIDE

By J. Yogerst

TOURS: There are essentially two ways of seeing Vietnam: as part of a guided group or as an individual. The sixteen-year travel ban imposed by the United States government ended in 1991, so it's now possible for American travel agents to book flights, hotels, and tours

Two reputable American agents with Vietnam travel programs are Abercrombie & Kent in Oak Park, Illinois, and Mountain Travel in Albany, California. The world's most experienced Vietnam tour operator is Diethelm Travel in Bangkok (Kian Gwan Building II, 40/1 Wireless Road, Bangkok 10330; tel: 255-9150/9160/9170), which is a five-minute walk from the Vietnam Embassy. Diethelm offers a number of tour options at very reasonable prices.

Thousands of foreign tourists fly to Hanoi and Ho Chi Minh City each year without hotel reservations or a tour program. But be forewarned that authorities still discourage foreigners from traveling unescorted in the countryside.

GETTING THERE: Until recently it was relatively difficult to fly into Vietnam because many international carriers were afraid to breach the American boycott. But the transportation situation has changed drastically in the last few years.

Bangkok remains the number-one gateway, with numerous flights each week to both Hanoi and Ho Chi Minh City (Saigon) on such carriers as Hang Khong Vietnam, Thai International, and Air France. Another convenient way to reach either city is via Hong Kong on Cathay Pacific Airways. There is also direct service from Manila on Philippine Airlines, from Kuala Lumpur on Malaysian Airlines, from Singapore on Singapore Airlines and Lufthansa, and from Jakarta on Garuda.

VISAS: All visitors must be in possession of a valid visa, which can be obtained from any Vietnamese diplomatic mission overseas. Most visitors get their visa upon arrival in Bangkok, at the Vietnam Embassy on Wireless Road. Tourist visas take twenty-four hours to process. Three passport-sized photos are required and there is a fee of U.S. $14. You can obtain a visa upon arrival at Tan Son Nhut Airport in Ho Chi Minh City, but it will cost you significantly more than in Bangkok: U.S. $75 for the visa itself and U.S. $25 for a police chop.

There are also Vietnamese embassies in Tokyo, Manila, and Kuala Lumpur, as well as Paris, London, Rome, Bonn, and Stockholm. The only place to obtain a visa in the United States is at the Vietnam Mission to the United Nations in New York.

HEALTH: Precautions against malaria are strongly recommended. Consult your family doctor or local pharmacist for the specific type of antimalaria prophylaxis, but the most likely recommendation is Lariam (Mefloquine). If you are traveling outside the big cities, inoculation against tetanus, cholera, typhoid, and hepatitis are also recommended.

It's also a good idea to pack your own small medical kit consisting of bandages, aspirin, antiseptic spray or cream, antihistamine cream, salt and water purification tablets, antidiarrhea medication, and a course of oral antibiotics. It is best to stick to bottled mineral water and refrain from eating ice and uncooked vegetables. The only hotel in Vietnam with its own water purification system is the Saigon Floating Hotel.

CLOTHING: During the summer months you can get by on shorts and a simple cotton shirt just about anywhere in Vietnam. But take a light sweater if you're going to be spending any time in highland areas—it gets chilly at night. The south remains blissfully warm during the winter, but Hanoi and other northern destinations can be awfully cold. If you're traveling in the north from October through March be advised to pack a thick sweater, several pairs of trousers, and some sort of jacket.

Vietnamese peasants are not used to seeing Western women in shorts. So if you don't want to offend local sensibilities, it's advisable to wear a skirt or long pants when traveling in the countryside.

Choice of footwear depends on the time of year and your itinerary. A good pair of walking shoes with rubber soles is the best bet, but a pair of rubber or leather sandals is good for wearing around the hotel or to the beach.

OTHER ITEMS: Besides the usual items you would take on any journey (toothbrush, shampoo, and so on) there are several other items you should take to Vietnam. Your own supply of toilet paper and facial tissues is highly recommended. Insect repellent is vital if you are going to be spending any time outside the cities. A small flashlight is a good idea, given the chronic blackouts that occur throughout Vietnam. For the same reason, it's best to leave the electrical appliances at home.

Bring along a small umbrella or raingear for the occasional wet weather. Conversely, both high-factor sun screen and a hat will keep you from frying in the intense tropical heat. You can purchase print film in Hanoi and Ho Chi Minh City, but it's better to purchase your camera supplies before leaving home or in Hong Kong or Bangkok.

GETTING AROUND: If you are part of a guided tour, you don't have to worry about domestic transport. Independent travelers will find it a constant hassle.

One of the best (and easiest) ways to see Vietnam is to take the train between Hanoi and Ho Chi Minh City. You can go straight through in about fifty-four hours, or make arrangements to stop off in cities like Hue, Danang, and Nha Trang along the way. There are two classes and sleepers are available. Expect to pay about U.S. $120 one way.

Hang Khong Vietnam Airlines has a domestic network serving Hanoi, Ho Chi Minh City, Danang, and Dalat. However, the Russian-made planes used by the airline are often in need of spare parts and aviation fuel is a rare and expensive commodity, so delays and cancellations are frequent.

There is a comprehensive system of intercity buses. These are theoretically off limits to foreigners, but many young travelers take buses without any problems. The same is true of rural taxis, which are most often old black French sedans or American cars and vans from the

1960s. Fares for both buses and taxis are dirt cheap, but the journey will be long, hot, and extremely uncomfortable. You can hire boats on some waterways, like the Perfume River in Hue and the Mekong River in Can Tho. But otherwise, water transport is a rather haphazard affair that requires a good working knowledge of Vietnamese.

Another option is hiring your own vehicle. Your hotels can recommend a local car-rental agency. Most of them are government agencies that compete against one another for tourist traffic. The prices are high, about U.S. $100 a day for a car and driver. But this cost can be shared by however many people are taking the journey with you. Try to get a new Japanese sedan or van—they cost more, but the air conditioning and modern shock absorbers make it worth every extra cent.

Most Vietnamese cities are small and compact enough to tour by foot. But a delightful alternative is the *cyclo* or pedal rickshaw. There are hundreds of cyclo drivers in Hanoi and Ho Chi Minh City, many of them military veterans. Many of them speak English and will gladly take you anywhere in the city center for the equivalent of several U.S. dollars.

MONEY: You can pay for just about anything in Vietnam with U.S. dollars—and sometimes you can even get old American coins as change! Travelers checks will do fine in the big cities where banks and hotels will change them, but you will need cash in the countryside and most urban shops.

Bring lots of ones and fives for smaller transactions. The Vietnamese *dong* continues to slide against the dollar and other Western currencies. It is illegal to change money on the black market, and not really necessary nowadays because the bank rate isn't that much different from the street.

Credit cards are a new phenomenon. Most hotels in Ho Chi Minh City and Hanoi now accept them, but few restaurants or shops take plastic. International Visa and Master Cards are your best bet; American Express and other U.S.-issued cards are not valid in Vietnam. And remember that it is virtually impossible to get money wired to you inside Vietnam.

HOTELS: There is just one Western-style, luxury/business hotel in all of Vietnam: the Saigon Floating Hotel, which is managed by the Australian-based Park Royal Group, a subsidiary of Hyatt. But that doesn't mean the other hotels are necessarily bad. There are a number of good French colonial-era abodes that are among the finest of their type in Asia. The Continental (Dong Khoi), Rex (Ben Thanh), and Majestic (Cuu Long) hotels in Ho Chi Minh City all offer superb standards of service, including spanking clean rooms, modern plumbing, and excellent restaurants. The elegant, old Metropole Hotel in Hanoi is currently under renovation.

All of the big tourist centers have at least one good, moderately priced hotel. The Perfume River (Huong Giang) Hotel in Hue has a brand new wing, but other accommodation in the city is basic. Danang has a good downtown hotel and a Soviet-style resort called the Non Nuoc at the south end of China Beach. The Palace Hotel in Dalat retains much of its French colonial charm. Try the recently renovated Hai Yen Hotel facing the beach in downtown Nha Trang.

Elsewhere the choice is meager. Every city and town has a government guest house, but the quality of these can vary greatly depending on the manager or the provincial bureaucrats who oversee these facilities. Vietnam's national oil company runs a string of resort hotels along the coast, but these also vary widely in terms of service, cleanliness, and cuisine.

Hotel rates range from about U.S. $100 a night for a single at the Saigon Floating Hotel to less than U.S. $15 a night for a double in a provincial guest house.

FOOD: The restaurant business is booming all over Vietnam. The economic liberalization of the late 1980s prompted many people to open their own eateries, ranging from modest *com pho* noodle stalls to fancy French cafés with candles and wine.

Hanoi has a number of interesting restaurants. Cha Ca has been a Hanoi institution for more than twenty years. The house specialty is a delicious fried rice and fish dish. The Piano Bar is relatively new, but already popular with both expatriate workers and tourists. Restaurant 202 is also popular with travelers. One of the best new cafés in Hanoi is the Viet Phuong Restaurant at 4 Mai Hac De Street, which has such specialties as eel soup, snails dipped in garlic and pepper sauce, soft-shelled crab, and roast rabbit.

It's hard to keep up with the rapid expansion of the food industry in Ho Chi Minh City. New restaurants seem to open every week. One of the best is Le Mekong, a rather pricey French café that features white linen tablecloths, silver settings, an extensive wine list (for Vietnam), waiters in black dinner jackets, and live entertainment each evening. La Bibliothèque Restaurant has an old-world charm that's straight out of a Graham Greene novel. The restaurants in the Rex and Majestic hotels are both very good. The old Arc-en-Ciel Restaurant in the Cholon section of Ho Chi Minh City is famous for its beef dishes, while the floating restaurants along the Saigon River offer sumptuous fish courses.

COMMUNICATIONS: Vietnam is rushing to modernize its telecommunications system, but it's not an easy task given its age and decrepit state. All overseas calls are routed via Bangkok and the overtaxed Thai telephone network, so even if you do manage to reach home it will sound as if you're talking to the dark side of the moon.

Large and medium hotels offer international call service from the front desk or a special kiosk; the only hotel with international direct dialing (IDD) from the guest rooms is the Saigon Floating Hotel. Main branch post offices also offer overseas telephone service.

Most hotels can also dispatch faxes and telexes, as can the larger post offices. Due to the poor overseas lines, faxes and telexes often arrive incomplete or garbled. You may have to send the message several times before it is relayed in toto.

GRATUITIES: No one wants to encourage outright begging, but like anywhere in the world it's a good idea to reward people for small services rendered. These can be modest gifts, like a cigarette in return for street directions. American smokes have been highly prized since all foreign tobacco was banned in 1990. Good gifts for children are pens, pencils, crayons, cartoon postcards, and chewing gum. T-shirts and baseball caps are also much appreciated.

GUIDE BOOKS: For further practical information on traveling in Vietnam you should consult *The Vietnam Guidebook* by Barbara Cohen (Harper & Row), recently updated in a second edition, *Guide to Vietnam* by John R. Jones (Bradt Publications), *Insight Guide to Vietnam* (Apa Publications), and *Vietnam: A Travel Survival Kit* (Lonely Planet).

INDEX

Italic page numbers indicate information in captions.